THE LENNON SISTERS

The Lennon Sisters

SWEETHEARTS OF SONG

A. H. PARR

Introduction by LAWRENCE WELK

DOUBLEDAY & COMPANY, INC.

GARDEN CITY, NEW YORK

1960

46034

Library of Congress Catalog Card Number 60–7880

Contents

Contents

Introduction

Ever since early childhood, my life has been bound up closely with the exciting world of music. It has been my good fortune to know most of the great musicians in the popular field for the last quarter century and more.

It has been a privilege and a joy to have known them. With these artists—needless to say—I include those who have been associated with my organization. They have been almost without exception persons of fine character, a credit to the world of entertainment, to their profession, and to their country.

Not all of them have been famous, or even successful. This business of music demands tremendous sacrifices for its great rewards. Natural talent is rarely enough by itself; a gifted person must expect years of hard work, of self-denial, even of hardships and heartbreaking disappointments. There are few exceptions. When you hear an accomplished musician, the chances are overwhelming that he has won his position through his own hard work and dauntless spirit.

Through the years I have heard many aspiring young musicians. Hundreds certainly, probably thousands. All were talented to a greater or lesser degree. But most of them simply did not have that little extra something which says, unmistakably, "Stardom!"

So it's a genuine pleasure for me to meet a youngster who has everything—talent, eagerness, beauty, warm-heartedness, a genuine desire to work and learn, an out-pouring, contagious personality. Imagine my delight when I met four of them at once!

Meeting the Lennon girls—Dianne, Peggy, Kathy, and Janet—and their family was one of the nicest things that ever happened to me. I met them almost by accident, a very lucky accident, and they have been a joy ever since. That they had talent and the kind of personality that's needed for success I knew immediately; but it wasn't until I had been acquainted with them for a while that I fully appreciated the fine qualities of the girls' characters: their warm family feeling, their happiness in bringing pleasure to others, their devotion to their work.

Let me add that I take no particular credit for having "discovered" these girls. They were bound to have been found, sooner or later, but it was my good fortune to have been there and to have had the joy of introducing them to the millions who listen to them each week.

They have made their way into the hearts of all of the musicians and staff members of the Welk organization. They are friends, daughters, and kid sisters all in one, and they fill this difficult role to perfection. The peace and goodness which you, as a member of the television audience, have felt flowing from them is not just a theatrical personality which they can take off or put on at will. That's the way they are.

Well, that's enough from me. Read and enjoy the book. I'm sure it will bring the four girls and their family even closer to you than they are now.

Lawrence Welk

THE LENNON SISTERS

CHAPTER I

The Magic Phone Call

One evening, late in the fall of 1955, the telephone rang in the home of Bill Lennon in Venice, California.

This, of itself, was not remarkable. Bill and his wife Isabelle—known to all as Sis—had plenty of friends, and the phone was likely to ring at any hour of the day. Also, they had four daughters, ranging in age from nine to fifteen; and as any parent knows, girls of that age and telephones are inseparable.

But this phone call was special. Of course, none of the Lennons knew it at the time, but that phone call was to change the course of their whole lives. It would take four happy, home-loving girls and put them up among the greatest stars of the entertainment world. Within a few short years the faces and the voices of the four Lennon sisters would be as familiar as those of close friends to the 30 million people who watch them over television each week.

They probably would have made it to the top, even without that fateful telephone call. Talent such as theirs is hard, even impossible, to keep in obscurity. But as it happened, the call was the thing that triggered the whole series of events that gave the country the Lennon sisters.

That was an important phone call.

Up until then, the evening had been an ordinary one. After dinner Dianne, as usual, began gathering up the dinner dishes to wash. "Come on, kids," she said to her younger sisters. "Cleanup time!"

Peggy, fourteen, and nearly two years younger than Dianne, looked woebegone. She gave a tentative cough. "DeeDee, maybe I shouldn't do dishes tonight. I think I have a cold coming on, and——"

"Nothing doing!" Dianne (DeeDee) said briskly. "Last night it was a sore finger, Peggy, and the night before that something else. Anything to get out of dishes!"

"But there are so many!" Peggy wailed, looking at the stacks of dishes on the big dining-room table. "DeeDee, I'll make your bed and sweep the floor, but you know how I hate dishes."

The third sister, Kathy, shook her head solemnly. "Don't you feel sorry for her, Janet? Isn't it awful? Poor Peggy!"

Little Janet, an eight-year-old pixie, only giggled and began collecting her share of the dinner dishes. Peggy's dismay was understandable. Two parents, four girls, and three little boys did use an amazing amount of china and silverware in the course of one dinner. And nobody really liked washing them. But it had to be done and the girls went about it with a cheerful efficiency—even Peggy, who went through the same performance every night and never got anywhere with it.

Water ran and suds mounted in the pan. "Say it isn't so . . ." DeeDee began to hum softly. "Say it isn't so . . ." Peggy's favorite song. Perhaps DeeDee chose it to soothe her sister's feelings. "Say it isn't so . . ." Her voice rose clear and sweet. The other girls joined in and the song became four-part harmony as the girls experimented with the chords, trying out this key and that one, their voices blending perfectly in a haunting arrangement of the popular tune.

Singing while they did dishes was an old custom with the Lennon girls. None of them, even gentle DeeDee, liked swishing around in the suds, and to make the time pass they had begun to sing together. First DeeDee and Peggy, later Kathy, and last of all, little Janet.

They went from one song to another easily, almost seeming to read each other's minds. Never a false note, never a faltering tone or a missed beat. True musicians, these girls, in spite of the fact that none of them could read music. The melodies were there, in their pretty heads. All they had to do was open their mouths and let the song float out.

Then Janet scooped up a handful of suds from the pan, held them under her chin like a white beard and began, "Santa Claus is coming to town . . ."

The others laughed. "Crazy!" DeeDee said affectionately, flipping a drop of water at her sister. "Let's get finished and have a game of ball."

Time for one more song. Kathy began "Down by the Old Mill Stream"; then as the others joined in she deliberately hit a flat note, throwing the whole thing into a doleful minor key.

A howl of dismay came from the front room, where their father was sitting, and all the girls laughed. "Ouch!"

Bill called. "Whoever did that is going to get permanent K.P.!"

"All through," DeeDee announced. "Janet, hang up your apron. No, not on the floor! Who's for a ball game?"

They tumbled through the front door and into the street.

The after-dishes ball game was almost as much of a tradition as the singing. Dianne, usually quiet and reserved, loved the shouting and rough-and-tumble of touch football or softball. So did the others, although they couldn't touch DeeDee's ability—except possibly Janet, a natural athlete.

"I'm going to be Ted Williams tonight!" Janet called, capering into the street waving the bat. "DeeDee can be Stan Musial and Kathy can be Mickey Mantle and . . ."

"And I'll be the Hitless Wonder, as usual," said Peggy. So the ball game began. Usually Bill Lennon joined in and often the girls' mother did too, while two of the little boys hopped up and down on the sidelines. But tonight Bill was tired—it's no easy job being a dairy salesman, with a vast territory to cover—and decided to sit quietly with his newspaper. Sis joined him, with the sewing, which is endless to a mother of seven children.

Quiet in the house, uproar in front where the girls played softball and Danny and Pat watched. Baby Bill was still too little to take much of an interest even in such a display of skill as his sisters playing ball.

In the newspaper was an item. Bill Lennon read: a noted TV singer had just signed a new contract guaranteeing him a fabulous salary for years to come. Bill closed his eyes and leaned back in the chair.

That might have been I, he reflected. Wonder what it would be like to be getting $5,000 a week?

He'd dreamed of it once. And the dreams hadn't been mere fancy either. It hadn't been so very long ago that the Lennon brothers had been one of the top singing groups on the West Coast; four of them, with Bill as lead tenor. No lack of bookings either. Vaudeville, supper clubs, dates with big name bands. As long ago as the late forties, Bill and his brothers had been with one of the greatest—Paul Whiteman's radio program. Bill had sung solo in the great Hollywood Bowl before a hushed audience of thousands. Supposing, supposing he had gone on with it? Where would he be today?

Bill looked around the room. Not shabby, but not luxurious either. The house looked lived in—homey and comfortable. But the armchair was worn, and there was a little threadbare spot on the carpet, and the baby had thrown blocks on the old sofa. He let his fancy wander a bit. Instead of Venice, perhaps Beverly Hills, or better yet one of the larger homes in Venice. They could never leave Venice where so many intimate friends and relatives lived—the town which held memories dear to their hearts, and the ocean only a few hundred yards away. For a minute he pictured himself in a mansion on a hilltop, sitting by his swimming pool in the evening and watching the million lights come on in the valley below, while the red sun sank over the mighty Pacific.

He shook his head. No, not for Bill Lennon. He'd made his choice, back in 1939; home and family instead of show business and travel. And not for a single minute had he regretted it. What did he lack that a contract for $5,000 a week would give him? A swimming pool? Why, he had the whole measureless Pacific in his back yard! A butler, maybe, cold and courteous, and a cook, and an expensive car?

Bill smiled. The picture didn't fit him at all. And what did he have that the $5,000-a-week singer didn't have? A wonderful wife—he looked fondly at Sis, sitting with her pretty head bent over the sewing. Four fine girls. Three little boys. Another baby coming, a baby who would be as welcome as the others had been. A happy home, where faith and love were the rule. Would he change places with the TV singer? The thought was so absurd that he laughed aloud, and Sis looked up with an inquiring glance.

Then the phone rang.

"I'll get it, honey," Bill said, getting up.

There was a boy on the other end of the wire, a boy who asked to speak to Dianne. "This is Larry," the boy said. "I'm a classmate of Dianne's."

"All right, Larry. She's playing ball out in the street. Wait a minute." He went to the front door and called her. "It's Larry," he said. "I didn't get his last name."

DeeDee bounced into the house, flushed and breathless from the ball game. "Must be Larry Welk," she said.

Bill had heard her speak of Larry, whose father was the orchestra leader. Odd, that the boy should call just as he was reading about a television singer.

DeeDee plumped down on a chair and picked up the receiver. "Hi," she said breathlessly.

"Hi, DeeDee. What did you do, just hit a home run?"

She giggled. "Not exactly. As a matter of fact, I struck out. I never can hit Janet's pitching—my little sister."

"Oh." There was a short moment of silence, then Larry said, "What I called about, DeeDee, the movie *Oklahoma* is being shown in Los Angeles Friday night and I wondered if you'd like to go."

"Friday? Gee, Larry, I'd love to, but we have a date Friday. I mean a date for singing," she explained in a rush. "My three sisters and I are singing at the Elks Club dance."

"Singing?" Larry said doubtfully. "I didn't know you sang."

"Oh, yes," DeeDee said. "We sing a little. You know, at meetings and things."

"Uh-huh," Larry said. He knew all about singing. Ever since he had been a baby, it was a rare moment in the Welk home when someone wasn't singing or playing something or listening to music. "Well, that's nice, Dee-Dee."

The conversation languished. DeeDee heard Peggy, from the street, yodeling for her to come back and finish the game. "I'm sorry, Larry," she said again.

"Well—listen, DeeDee," said Larry suddenly. "What time is your show over?"

"Gosh, I don't know exactly. Probably around ten o'clock. Maybe a little later. Why?"

"I was thinking I could meet you at the Elks Club when you're through and then we could go to the show."

"Why," she said slowly, "I'd like to, if my parents say it's O.K. Wait a minute, Larry." She covered the phone and turned to her parents, asking their permission.

"Well . . ." Bill was a little dubious. It would mean Dianne would be out quite late, and she was, after all, only fifteen. Still, Larry Welk was a nice boy, from all reports, and certainly his father's reputation was tops. Bill looked at Sis, and they both looked at DeeDee. Her eyes were bright, with a pleading look. Sis smiled and nodded.

"All right, DeeDee," Bill said.

"It's all right!" she reported happily to Larry. "I can go, Larry, and thanks for asking. See you at the Elks Club Friday."

She jumped to her feet and whirled out of the room, calling the news to Peggy, Kathy, and Janet, who were still playing softball.

And that, as you might think, was that. A pretty fifteen-year-old girl accepting a date to a movie with a classmate. How many times a week does that happen in the United States? A few hours of laughter and conversation, a day of giggling discussion, and it's forgotten.

But this was the date that really started something. What if Larry Welk had decided to ask someone else, or if DeeDee had had a date with another boy that Friday, or if the Lennons hadn't had a singing engagement, or if her parents had decided against it?

But Larry didn't and DeeDee hadn't and the Lennons had and the parents didn't, and so it all worked out— beautifully.

One more thing: suppose Larry hadn't suddenly decided that he might as well get to the Elks Club a little early so he could hear the girls?

But he did. He heard them, all right.

Young Larry Welk showed up at the Elks Club as he had promised. But he got there at nine when the program was due to start—not at ten, when Dianne would be finished.

It would be hard to explain why he came there early. Certainly it wasn't in any great expectation of seeing a wonderful show. A child of show business himself, he had picked up the habit of judging a performance by professional standards, and he didn't expect to be knocked out of his seat, even speaking metaphorically. He knew club entertainments, too, and could almost have predicted what would be on the program:

A magician not quite good enough to get theater or night-club bookings. A young man who played the guitar and sang. A girl—or possibly two girls—who did a tap dance to the music of "Tea for Two." A sugary tenor who sang a popular standard ballad, or an even more sugary soprano with a tendency to wabble and fade above high C. Maybe a ventriloquist, a male quartet calling itself "The Hi-Boys" or some such title, a trombonist imitating Dorsey—the possibilities were almost limitless and not at all encouraging.

Still, he went to the Elks Club dance.

Larry arrived at the Elks Club early. All around him was the murmur and babble of voices as people greeted friends. Late comers were still arriving, pausing to wave at fellow Elks. Larry sighed and wriggled down a little in his hard chair. Not a smart move coming so early to this thing, he told himself, and for a minute wondered what had impelled him. The answer to that was obvious: the prospect of a date with pretty DeeDee Lennon, with her wide blue eyes fringed by dark lashes—the Irish look, Larry called it. Not that this was any great romance, or anything. He liked her, in a friendly boy-girl way, and enjoyed her company. That was all. It would be fun to take her on a date and introduce her to his parents. He was looking forward to it.

Now there was a bustle on the stage. A smiling man came out to be met by a spatter of applause and a few shouted greetings. He held up his hand and launched into a speech: "Ladies, fellow Elks, and honored guests . . ."

There Larry lost him. His attention wandered. Odd, he'd never known that DeeDee sang. In some girls' chorus, he supposed. Maybe a church choir, although it wasn't likely that a church choir would appear on a club program. She'd said her three sisters. Larry thought he'd met one once—Peggy, he remembered her name was, a pretty little thing with dark brown eyes instead of blue ones.

Applause rose again, together with a rippling murmur of the kind women give when they see something pretty or cute. Larry blinked. Those four girls—— Sure, they were! The Lennons!

A quartet, and he hadn't even heard the master of ceremonies announce them! He sat straighter in his chair. There was Dianne, second from the right, and Peggy and two other girls he hadn't met. All dressed alike.

The four voices rose, so closely blended it was impossible to distinguish notes or to tell who was singing what. Larry leaned forward with a little stirring of excitement. The girlish, sweet voices filled the hall. Everyone was quiet, everyone was leaning forward, listening and watching raptly.

"Come to me, bend to me . . ." They were singing a

lovely air from the musical comedy *Brigadoon*, a Scottish wedding song sung in the mysterious, enchanted village that comes to life only once every hundred years.

"Darling, my darling, it's all I can say . . ." Looking around, Larry saw unashamed tears in more than one eye. He himself felt that pang of—what can it be called? The tightening in the throat which tells you that you are seeing or hearing something very beautiful.

They finished, holding the last note in true pitch, letting it die away gradually, fading as the enchanted village of the song faded. There was a second or two of silence, than a roar of applause.

The girls smiled and bowed, gracefully but a little shyly. Then they began to sway and launched into another song. This time it had a gay, happy lilt that had the whole audience swaying and smiling with them.

And to think—Larry told himself wryly—that I was picturing them as amateurs! Why, plenty of professional singers have tried out for Dad's orchestra who weren't nearly that good. Not half as good! Dad's orchestra . . . H'm. An idea hit him. But no use rushing things. He'd think about it a little first.

After the show DeeDee came over to him, her blue eyes sparkling and her light brown pony-tail bouncing. "Hi!" she said. "Were you here when we sang? I didn't know you were going to come to the show."

"Hey, slow down!" he laughed. "Yes, I heard you and I thought you were swell."

"Gee," DeeDee said. "Thanks!" She appreciated the compliment, coming from Larry Welk, who knew good music when he heard it.

He took her arm. "Well, shall we go?"

The show *Oklahoma* was good and they both enjoyed it. DeeDee usually has a good time no matter what she does. And people who are with her have fun too—she is that kind of girl. Not a word did Larry say all evening about the scheme which was buzzing around in his head, but the more he thought about it, the better he liked it. What the heck, there wouldn't be any harm in trying! He'd wait until Sunday, after Mass. In his dad's hard-working life, Sunday morning was one of the few times he could relax.

So, on Sunday morning, Larry came into the living room where his dad sat with the Sunday paper spread out around him.

"I took DeeDee Lennon to the show Friday," he said, in what he hoped was a casual tone. "I don't think you ever met her, did you, Dad? She's a swell girl."

"Um," said his father. Larry knew that tone of old. Translated, it meant: "I'm always glad to hear about what you're doing, son, but right now I'm reading about another television show." Amazing, how much adults could put into one syllable when they were concentrating on another subject. He was a little dashed. But just then his mother and sister Donna came in. Maybe he could talk to them and his dad would kind of hear. "You know DeeDee Lennon, don't you, Sis?"

"Sure," Donna said. "She's your current big thing, isn't she?"

"Don't tease, Donna," her mother said. "DeeDee is a lovely girl."

That was Larry's opening. Enthusiastically he launched

into a description of the Elks Club program; how the Lennon sisters quartet had held the audience breathless, how great they were, how each of the sisters had absolute tone—that rare quality of being able to find the proper note and sing it perfectly, without effort.

"I think Dad ought to hear them," he finished. Turning to his father, he said hopefully, "Don't you, Dad?"

Welk looked up. "Don't I what?"

Larry sighed. He hadn't heard a word! He tried again. "DeeDee Lennon sings in a quartet with her three sisters. They sang Friday night at an Elks Club program and they were just wonderful! I was telling Mother you should hear them."

"Sure, son," Welk said. "Someday I'll hear them, maybe." He turned to his wife. "Fern, should we go to the Rose Bowl game this year?"

Well, he'd tried. Of course, Larry couldn't blame his dad. As with all top orchestra leaders, he was besieged day after day, year in and year out, with throngs of hopeful singers and instrumentalists. Some of the top professionals in the country had asked for tryouts with the Welk orchestra—and were still on a waiting list. The orchestra manager had a file of applicants numbering hundreds, maybe thousands. Two men who worked for his dad did nothing but listen to recordings of hopeful young musicians whose dream in life was to play or sing with Lawrence Welk.

Larry had heard lots of those records and listened to many of the musicians in person. And he had to admit some of them were pretty awful. Singers who lost the rhythm, or hit wrong notes. Trumpet players who cracked.

Saxophonists with a thin, reedy tone. Quartets who were just—well, just amateurs, all right for a party in somebody's house but out of their depth among professionals.

How could his father know that the Lennons weren't just four more kids who wanted to be stars? Actually, now that he stopped to think about it, Larry wasn't even sure that the girls were interested in show business. He sighed again. Maybe he'd just better forget the whole thing. No! I'm not a real musician, he said to himself. But I've been around music so long I think I can tell what's good and what isn't. And those girls are good! Dad's going to hear them!

During the next two weeks, Larry campaigned for the Lennons. Not openly. But sometimes it seemed to Fern Welk, Larry's mother, that she was hearing a great deal about DeeDee Lennon and her sisters. Larry would drop a remark casually at dinner, or in the evening when the family was together. All the remarks had much the same theme: "Someday some lucky orchestra leader is going to hear those Lennons sing. Then watch them go!"

It was a little discouraging. His father never asked about them—never even seemed to hear.

But then, about two weeks after the Elks Club show, on a Sunday early in December, Lawrence Welk, Senior, woke up sneezing, with eyes watering and a sore throat.

Fern looked at him closely and said lovingly, "You've been driving yourself too hard! I knew you'd get sick! Now you stay in bed and rest. I'll take the children to church."

"I'll go to an early Mass and then to bed," replied Lawrence.

After Mass he went to bed but not for long. Cold or no cold, Welk was too active to spend the day lolling in bed, with so much to be done. He got up and dressed and put on a recording the orchestra had made that week. He wasn't quite satisfied with it, but he didn't know exactly why. Maybe if he listened a few times . . .

He played the recording over and over, finally deciding the brass didn't have quite enough bounce and vitality, and the rhythm was falling apart. They'd have to try again. It wouldn't do to press a record that wasn't up to the Welk standard.

He wasn't feeling as miserable as he had earlier when he heard Larry and Donna come back from church. Then Welk smiled. He had an idea. "Larry," he called. "Come here a minute, will you?"

His son poked his head in the doorway. "You call me, Dad?"

"Yes. I've been hearing complaints from your mother."

Larry looked bewildered. "Complaints?"

"She says all she's heard out of you for the past two weeks are hymns of praise about these girls you heard sing the other night. What's their name? Donnelly? Svenstrom? MacIntyre?"

"Lennon! I thought you'd forgotten all about them!"

His father laughed. "I'm like an elephant, son. I never forget. Least of all anything that has to do with music. Well, you said you'd like me to hear them. Here I am, home sick"—he gave a hollow cough to show how sick he was—"and nothing to do. Do you suppose the girls could come over this afternoon and show me what they can do? What's their name again? O'Malley?"

27

"Lennon—as if you didn't know!" Larry was beaming. "Are you kidding?"

"No, of course not. If you recommend them, son, that's all I want to know. Go call your friend and see."

"Here I go!" shouted Larry happily, beginning to run off.

"Son . . ."

"Yes, Dad?"

"You're not—I mean, you don't have a crush on this girl, do you?" Welk was serious.

"A crush?" Larry grinned. What a phrase! Crush! "No, of course not. I like her, but that's all. Why?"

"Well, son, I'll be glad to listen to them, especially since you think they're good. I rely on your judgment. But just remember: I won't flatter them, or give them false hopes, or anything like that, just because one of the girls is a friend of yours. I'll judge their singing just as impartially as if they'd come to me without any recommendation at all. I want you to understand. I just don't want your feelings hurt—or theirs either."

"Why, sure, Dad! I understand that!" Of course, he didn't want any special consideration for the Lennons. And he knew his father well enough to know that his verdict would be fair—stern, maybe, but fair. He waved and started for the telephone, grinning again. Crush! Brother! He'd have to remember that.

And so it came about that two hours later the four Lennon sisters—excited, a little awed, but not at all frightened—arrived with their parents at the Welk home, after driving in a downpour of rain.

A somewhat flustered Larry let them in, ushered them

into the living room, and introduced the Lennons to the Welks and Mr. and Mrs. Ed Spaulding. Mr. Spaulding is Lawrence Welk's business manager. Then Larry retired to a corner and sat down. It was out of his hands now—he had done what he could.

Lawrence Welk and Bill Lennon talked for a few minutes. They knew many of the same people, shared some of the same memories. After all, they were both professional artists, although one of them had forsaken his career. Then the orchestra leader said:

"Well, how about these four pretty girls of yours? My son tells me they're the greatest thing since the Rhythm Boys."

Dianne glared at Larry in mock anger, while the other three tried not to look excited or wriggle too much. Bill Lennon laughed.

"That was nice of Larry. But I think he's a little too enthusiastic. Still . . ." His pride in his four daughters overcame his reluctance to boast about them. "Still, I think they're pretty good, myself." He nodded at the girls.

Quietly, without any feigned restraint or fuss, DeeDee, Peggy, Kathy, and little Janet got up and stood together. They knew—as Peggy had said when they left home—"This is it!" If Lawrence Welk liked them, if he thought they could go places, why—there wasn't any place they couldn't go. He might call some agents or people in the business, and get them some bookings. He might even (this was just dreaming) have them for a guest spot on his television show. Their only desire was to make some money to help Dad and Mother. Janet had said this, jumping up and down, but quiet DeeDee had only hugged her and said, "Don't start building castles in the air, Janny. Let's just sing our best and pray."

They had all prayed, humbly and silently. Not for wealth or fame, but just for a chance to help Dad and Mother and the little boys. Daddy and Mother worked so hard!

And the Lennon sisters began their first song for Lawrence Welk. It was the beautiful spiritual, "He." The favorite song of Kathy—funny, dreamy Kathy, the girl with stardust in her eyes, the girl who loved little children even more than she loved to sing.

"He can turn the tides and calm the angry sea,
He, alone, decides who writes a symphony.
He lights every star that makes our darkness bright,
He keeps watch all through each long and lonely night."

No tricks, no phony stage smiles, no artificial attempts to impress anybody. Just four sisters, girls with clear, true voices, singing a great song the way the song was written to be sung. The melody filled the room. It seemed to bring everyone sad dreams of things lovely and far away and wonderful.

The song ended. There was silence in the room.

After a moment Welk stirred and asked, "Do you girls know another song?"

He sounded, young Larry thought, not especially impressed or even interested. Larry's heart sank. He'd heard his dad sound the same way just before he'd shaken his head at others who had had auditions—not interested.

But the girls were singing again and he listened to their

harmonizing of "When we come of age . . ." Then they were finished, looking at his father half in hope, half in fear.

Lawrence Welk just sat there, calmly, saying nothing. The silence in the room grew until it seemed to fill every corner, as the girls' music had a moment earlier. Finally, Bill Lennon could bear it no longer. Trying to hide his deep concern, he asked:

"Well, what do you think?"

DeeDee clasped and unclasped her hands behind her back. Peggy, the most devout, offered a silent prayer. Kathy, unable to express herself any other way, wiggled her toes inside her shoes, and Janet tried to keep from hopping on one foot.

Finally, Welk smiled. "What do I think? Oh, yes. Why, I think . . ." Breathless, they waited. "I just can't believe my ears. I think I'd like someone else to hear them."

Someone else? The sisters, their parents, and the Welks looked at one another, a little puzzled, while he went to the phone. He dialed a number, then they heard him say:

"George? Hi! This is Lawrence. . . . Fine. . . ."

George—that was George Cates, Welk's musical supervisor, a man with almost uncanny ability to spot a potential star. Welk was speaking again.

"George, do you have a minute? I'd like to have you listen to a song over the phone. Four girls—a quartet."

George broke in to ask, "You don't mean to tell me you have the McGuire Sisters there, do you?"

"No," replied Lawrence. "They're the Lennon sisters.

31

No, you haven't heard of them. But you will, George, you will!"

He beckoned to the girls to come to the phone.

Outside the rain drenched the parched earth, singing a song of hope for the withering flowers and plants of the land. It whispered its heavenly blessing to the four wholesome youngsters inside, who were being born again in song, one which would stir the pulse of millions of young and old living in every city and hamlet of our great land.

When the song ended, Ed Spaulding came over to Lawrence. In an enthusiastic voice he asked, "What are you waiting for, Lawrence? Why don't you have them sing for your big Christmas show?"

CHAPTER II

A Night of Joy

On the ride home to Venice, through the soft rain of southern California, the girls started playing, as girls will, the old game of "Just suppose."

"Just suppose," Kathy said, "that Mr. Welk decided to have us on his show, and we're a big hit, and we get to be television singers, and . . ."

"Just suppose he doesn't," said Peggy, more practical. She sighed. "Still, it would be nice!"

Over and over, they relived the short time in the Welk home. Bubbling with excitement, the girls poured forth a torrent of talk. "I think he liked us, don't you, DeeDee? He phoned Mr. Cates, and Mr. Spaulding came over to us and said we sang very good. Isn't Larry nice? And Mrs. Welk told me not to worry. I thought we sounded all right, didn't you, Peggy? I wasn't a bit scared, only just a little nervous! Not scared? Why, Janet, I could see your knees knocking together right through your dress!"

And so on, until finally Sis Lennon said gently: "Girls, just remember: it doesn't matter so much whether anything comes of your audition or not. What matters is that you sang beautifully and Daddy and I are proud of you!"

"That's right," Bill said. "And I don't want you to feel

disappointed if you don't hear from Mr. Welk again. He's one of the biggest people in show business, and he hears hundreds of young singers every year. He has the best talent in the country to choose from. Promise me you won't worry, or build up your hopes too high."

"We promise," the four of them chorused. But it wouldn't have been human nature if they hadn't day-dreamed a little, or talked over all the possibilities as they lay in bed, whispering together and giggling.

Days went by with no word. True to their promise, the girls didn't bother their parents with fretting and fussing about whether Mr. Welk would call. But both Sis and Bill noticed that every time the phone rang, each girl within hearing distance turned her head to listen, with an expression half of fear, half of hope.

When the call turned out to be from some friend of the Lennons, and not Welk at all, a little sigh escaped them.

But, of course, the call came. A week after that rainy Sunday, the phone rang—and this time, sure enough, it was Lawrence Welk. To the four girls, standing around with their eyes big, Bill winked and nodded.

He talked only a few minutes. "Yes, Lawrence. . . . They're fine. . . . Why, thanks! Yes. . . . Yes. . . . Your Christmas show?"

The girls could fill in the gaps. Lawrence Welk was ask-ing them to sing on his Christmas show, one of the biggest shows of the television year, heard by millions of people!

The idea was too big for them to absorb all at once. DeeDee sank down on the davenport. Kathy and Peggy joined hands and began a sort of war dance until Bill signaled them to stop. Janet covered her mouth with her hands.

"Yes, Lawrence," Bill was saying. There was a quiver of excitement in his voice. "That would be fine. I know the girls will like it. They'll be ready. Yes, we'll all be there. Thanks again! Good-by."

He hung up the receiver and turned slowly. "You heard, girls?" They nodded. "Mr. Welk wants you to sing 'He' on his Christmas show. You all know it well, but you'll have to practice. . . ."

He got no further. Four girls couldn't hold in their excitement any longer. They hugged each other, Sis and Bill, and their little brothers, to the boys' disgust. They gave no thought to the money they would earn because they loved to sing; just being on the Lawrence Welk TV show would be fun, and they were anxious to make good for their parents' sake.

Then, being girls, they all asked simultaneously:

"What will we *wear*?"

Bill smiled. With a wife and four daughters, he knew how important such a decision could be, but it wasn't his department. Sis would have to decide that. She took charge.

"All right, let's figure out what you're going to wear. There isn't time for me to make dresses, so we'll have to buy something. You all want to be dressed alike, so it will have to be something that you agree on." Turning to her husband, she inquired, "Bill, is it all right to buy dresses for them?"

He thought of their slim bank account. The dresses

would have to be nice. Nothing cheap—not for the Welk Christmas show! He could trust Sis to make the wisest purchase.

"You're the boss of the costume department," he said. "I'll just be in the way."

He went to play with the little boys, leaving his wife and the four girls happily talking woman-talk about styles and materials. Wisely Sis let DeeDee take the lead. Dee-Dee, the oldest, had always shown excellent taste in clothes.

"Nothing too flowery or fancy," DeeDee said firmly, rejecting Janet's hopeful suggestion of cowboy outfits, or maybe spangles. "I think the simpler the better!"

Sis agreed wholeheartedly, although Kathy, only twelve then, spoke wistfully of clouds of net draperies, and Peggy, fourteen, suggested something glittery.

In the end the girls agreed with DeeDee's idea, sec- onded by their mother—navy-blue suits and white blouses. "All right," Janet sighed. "I guess you know best. But it would have been lovely to dress in white cowboy clothes!"

The next evening the whole family went shopping. This was a rare treat for the girls, whose mother usually made all their clothes.

Even Bill, who had the usual male reaction to shop- ping—acute torture—enjoyed himself, watching the girls get their outfits. Janet, as always, dashed around the store, dazzled by the displays and getting lost in the toy de- partment. It was a wonderful evening. The Christmas things were in, and the big store was like fairyland. It took all of Sis's firmness to keep the girls quiet long enough to try on the navy-blue suits.

At last, though, the four girls paraded before their parents. Bill squeezed his wife's hand. "I'll tell you a secret," he whispered. "We've got four mighty pretty daughters!"

Sis agreed. In their costumes, all alike, the girls looked lovely. Besides, she told herself, the navy-blue outfits would last a long time. Sis could not afford daydreams. It was wonderful that her daughters had a chance on a big-time show, but the show lasted one hour. And then what? Would there be more shows, or would that one be all? For the sake of her girls, she hoped there would be more. But in show business, you never knew.

The days passed in a round of rehearsals at home, combined with the usual routine of school and play. Again and again the girls told themselves that singing over a nationwide network was no different from singing on an Elks Club program. But in spite of that, they couldn't help feeling more and more nervous.

It wasn't so much that success would mean money, maybe a lot of money. That would be nice, of course, but mostly because it would help Mother and Dad build another room onto their small, overcrowded, two-bedroom home. The girls just didn't have any idea of what "a lot of money" meant. More playthings for the little boys, perhaps, or a new dress, or a sewing machine for Mommy.

Mostly they were anxious to make good for the sake of their parents, who had done so much for them. And besides, of course, the four girls just loved to sing, and it was a thrill to be singing with the famous Lawrence Welk orchestra.

Finally, the great day came! There are always a hundred last-minute things to do before a major network TV show goes on the air, and Welk, a man who believes in having everything exactly right, had asked them to be at the studio at seven in the morning.

It was still dark outside when the lights went on in the Lennon home. Janet yawned and grumbled a little: "Do we have to get up in the middle of the night?"

But in a few minutes they forgot about being sleepy. The excitement of the day caught them up. Sis had carefully made everything ready the night before, and the girls got dressed and ready with no more than the normal amount of confusion and chattering.

The night sky was just beginning to pale a little when the family left on the twenty-mile drive to the ABC Studios. Dianne rode in the front seat with her father, while Peggy, Kathy, and Janet sat in back. Sis, of course, had to stay home with the little ones.

She told them good-by, with a hug and kiss for each one. "I know you'll sing beautifully," she said. "Good luck! I'll be watching!"

"We'll sing 'specially for you," Dianne promised, and the others nodded.

There wasn't much traffic as Bill drove east on Venice Boulevard. As they approached Sepulveda Boulevard, a main intersection, the light flashed green. Bill, who had slowed down for the traffic signal, speeded up again. As he did he noticed a car coming from the east, going far too fast. It had no lights.

The other car didn't even slow down, although its driver must have seen the red light. It looked as if a smash-up was coming sure—as if the other car would plow right into the Lennons.

The girls screamed. Later Bill said:

"All kinds of things flashed through my mind. It had happened so suddenly I didn't really think, except 'We'll be late at the studio!'"

Instinctively he knew that braking wouldn't help. He jammed the gas pedal to the floor and the car leaped forward.

The other auto roared past behind them, inches away.

Bill, white and trembling, pulled in to the curb. The girls in the back seat were clutching each other in terror. He smiled, a little shakily, trying to calm them. "That was a close one!" he said.

"He ran the stop light!" Kathy said indignantly. "Yes, and without any lights!" said Dianne. Janet had a thought. "I betcha he's a robber. Maybe a bank robber!"

The others laughed, and their tension eased. "Say a prayer of thanks for safe deliverance," Bill told them, and the girls bowed their heads. "I'll pray to St. Christopher," Peggy said.

He started the car and they drove on. Nothing else happened, and they arrived at the big studios right on time. Even at that hour of the morning, the buildings were lighted and full of activity. Bill gave his name to the receptionist, and the man said:

"Yes, Mr. Welk told me to expect you. Right through that door."

Bill shepherded the girls into the huge studio. Awed and a little frightened, they kept close together. "Golly!" Dianne said.

The studio was a very large room, lighted only at one end. Myriads of spotlights, of all sizes, hung from the high ceiling. Men trundled scenery, racks of costumes, props, settings, around the floor. Other men worked with the big cameras. Still others hurried around with sheaves of papers, various kinds of equipment, and other things needed to put a show on the air. Dozens of monitor screens stood around. The orchestra was already in place, warming up by playing runs, trills, and melodies. A singer was running through her scales. Workmen shouted at each other as they placed the spotlights and planned camera angles.

Then Welk spotted them and came over, a wide smile on his face, his hand held out in welcome. "Hi!" he said. "How nice you look! All ready, Bill?"

"All ready," Bill said, shaking hands.

Now that Mr. Welk was here, the place no longer seemed strange to the girls. He led them to a place where they could watch all that was going on and asked a member of the ABC staff to explain things to them.

"I want you to meet the rest of the people on the show," Welk said. "You'll like them, and I know they'll like you."

One by one they came over—Myron Floren, Jerry Burke, Johnny Klein, Dick Kesner, Larry Hooper, and others until they had met everyone. Each shook hands with the girls and wished them the best of luck.

It was a long day, but an interesting one. The girls listened to the other numbers which would be on the show. "Golly," Peggy whispered, "we'd better be good! Listen to them!"

They ran through their song—"He," a reverent ballad

—by themselves, with the producers and directors listening critically. When they'd finished, everybody smiled and applauded, and the producer said:

"That's fine, girls, just fine! Nothing to worry about!"

They stood here, and there, and someplace else, as the director told them. Lights flashed up suddenly in their faces, making Janet blink. Men called to each other: "Bring 'em up a little! Move that smallest girl back—forward—a little more! That's it!"

It was somewhat confusing. But, as Welk told them, "If you're sure you have it just the way you want it before the show starts, it gives you confidence."

Finally, the director passed the word, "Fifteen minutes!"

The big studio grew quiet. Performers, technicians, and staff members waited for the word which would put the Lawrence Welk show on the air.

Ten minutes—five minutes—three minutes. Just before "on camera" is always an exciting, nerve-racking time. The girls tried to sit quietly, but they couldn't help a sinking feeling in the pit of their stomachs. "Just relax," their father told them. "Just forget all about the cameras and everything else. Go out there and sing the way you always have. Remember, Mother's watching."

Then, suddenly, everything seemed to happen at once. The show opened with Lawrence Welk's well-known "champagne music." A waltz—a ballad—a piano number. Then he was announcing them:

"It gives me the greatest pleasure to introduce to you four young ladies who are my friends and I know will be yours from now on. Here are Dianne, Peggy, Kathy, and

Janet—the Lennon sisters. They will sing the beautiful song, so fitting for this Christmas season, 'He.'"

Almost as if in a dream, the girls walked out to face the camera, Welk smiled encouragingly and gave them a friendly wink. He raised his baton. Then Jerry Burke, the organist, gave them a lead in arpeggio, and they sang their song unaccompanied by music, referred to in the world of music as *a cappella.*

Afterward, Dianne said that as soon as they began to sing, she felt perfectly at home. She is the calmest of the four girls, and her poise helps steady the others. Peggy and Kathy confessed they felt a little shaky, and little Janet, only nine, said, "My mouth was so dry! And my knees shook!"

The people in the studio and the millions watching over television didn't notice. They saw only four lovely young girls and heard only the sweet, tender voices blending in a song. There was more there than just harmony, careful phrasing and sweetness of tone. Through the song filtered the warmth, the happiness, and the love which had enfolded their lives since they could remember.

The song ended. A perfect torrent of applause filled the studio. Tears glistened in many eyes. The performers recognized real talent and their applause was loudest of all.

Hardly had the girls bowed and stepped from the stage than the phone in the studio began ringing. People wanted more! And when the hour-long show had ended, Welk and his musicians crowded around. "That was great!" "Congratulations!" "When are you coming again?"

"They'll be back," Welk said, smiling. He took the hands of each of the girls and pressed them between his own. "That was fine, just wonderful! And now we can all relax a little!"

The girls flew to the phone to call Mother. Of course she was happy and proud. "The little boys couldn't believe that it was their sisters there on the TV screen," she told Dianne. "Little Pat kept saying, 'That looks like Janet!'"

The girls could hardly believe it themselves. With the tension of the show behind them, the musicians and production staff mingled in an informal Christmas party. With the others, and again by themselves, the girls sang the ancient Christmas carols. The other members of Welk's staff went out of their way to make the girls feel at home. No professional jealousy there—no room for it in Welk's organization.

Then, later, on their way home again, the events of the great day whirled dizzily through the girls' heads. They were too tired to talk much. The four girls lay back quietly, each one thinking of what had happened.

Bill pulled up in front of the house. Janet stirred sleepily, lifting her head from Peggy's shoulder. As she stepped down from the car she said, "Gee! I'm tired. But singing on television sure is fun, isn't it?"

CHAPTER III

When Irish Eyes Are Smiling

That was, of course, only the beginning. In days to come the four Lennon girls would get used to the frantic bustle of a big TV studio, the endless search for perfection in rehearsals, the split-second timing.

Many phone calls had flooded into ABC's office after their song. Next day, and on succeeding days, Welk's phone continued to ring incessantly. Letters and telegrams poured in. Thousands of persons called, wrote, or wired, and they all asked the same thing:

"Where did you find those sweet Lennon girls? Are we going to see and hear them again?"

Welk heard the reports of the flood of mail and calls, and nodded. When first he had heard them, that rainy Sunday at his home, he had thought: "Here's something new. These girls could be a great hit!"

His instinct had been right. Welk is not often wrong in judging talent. He called in his manager:

"Let's get these girls signed up. We'll have them as a regular part of the program."

They were going places, and Welk knew they would be far better off under his sponsorship than by themselves. He could watch over them, protect them. They were, after all, just youngsters—they needed a guiding hand, and he felt he could give it to them.

The contract was prepared. It is difficult to sign a youngster to a contract in the state of California. First, it is necessary to get the approval of a court. Bill Lennon came in to sign on behalf of his daughters. The girls signed, too, of course, but oddly enough, it didn't seem to impress them much. Other girls might have had their heads turned by the prospect of fame, of making so much money, of being accepted on terms of equality by the top stars of television and the movies.

Well, just think: supposing you were offered a chance to mix with such people as Pat Boone, Dinah Shore, Jack Benny, Bing Crosby, Steve Allen, and dozens more? Supposing you were told your name would be as familiar to millions as theirs are? Wouldn't it make you a little giddy? Wouldn't you feel it was too good to be true?

Of course, the four Lennon girls were excited and happy. But—and this is the solemn truth—it didn't make much difference to their lives. It didn't make posturing puppets out of four nice girls, as it might have done. They still enjoy meeting stars—who wouldn't?—and they still feel a thrill when someone like Perry Como writes them a fan letter. But they don't think of themselves as "TV stars."

They go to rehearsals and shows; they make records; they tour the country making appearances; their names are in the papers; they are recognized on the streets or in stores and youngsters shyly ask for their autographs. And naturally, being human, they like it.

But still, their greatest delight is to be with their family.

Having the right home life, they do not seek other pleasures. They like to play with the baby, or sit and talk with a friend over the telephone, just as much as any of the countless teen-age girls the country over. They enjoy baseball games in the back yard as much as ever. Their ambitions are modest and may be summed up in a phrase: To lead a good life.

What's the answer? Simple!

Since the earliest days that Dianne, the eldest, can remember, the Lennon family has been a unit. Every member of it loves every other member. They just like to be together. This doesn't mean that they don't sometimes have their squabbles; every family does. Kathy gets mad at Peggy for wearing her new scarf—little things like that. It doesn't last though.

Love, and a sense of humor, can overcome most obstacles, and the Lennon family has both in full measure.

But where did they get their musical talent? Did it just appear, full blown, in the four girls?

By no means. On both sides of the family the girls have inherited a rich musical tradition. They are typically American; in their veins runs the blood of ancestors from Ireland, Germany, and Spain. Each has left its own legacy of music.

Lennon is an Irish name—so let's look first at the strain which comes down to the four girls from County Cork.

Just a few years before the Civil War, James and Mary Lennon, the progenitors of the Clan Lennon, came from Ireland in a sailing vessel. Those were bad days for the

47

Old Sod; the potato famine was driving hundreds of thousands of Irish across the sea.

John Lennon was born shortly after they settled in Appleton, Wisconsin, and in 1886 Herbert Lennon, known as Bert, John's son, was born there. The four Lennon sisters never saw their father's father, but nevertheless Grandpa Bert had a great influence on them through their own dad, Bill.

Bert grew up a tall lad, with flaming red hair and freckles. His neighbors said, with more truth than originality, that he had the map of Ireland on his face. He had inherited other things from the "Land of Saints and Scholars"—the gift of an eloquent, persuasive tongue, as if he had kissed the Blarney stone, and a musical singing voice. In high school he entered, and won, the state oratorical contest.

Bert discovered that his fluency with words extended to writing. He decided to become a newspaperman and went to work as a cub reporter for the Twin City Publications, St. Paul, Minnesota. This was a good apprenticeship, but hardly wide enough scope for a young man of his energy and ambition, and in the early years of the twentieth century he went to Chicago.

Chicago was then—and still is, for that matter—a live, energetic, exciting city. The big redhead from Wisconsin used his talent for talk—a hint of County Cork was still in his voice—to get a job as a dramatic critic and feature writer on Hearst's *Evening American*.

Being a newspaperman was exciting work, although hours were long and pay was poor. Still, there were plenty of compensations. After work, Bert and the other newsmen used to gather in one of the restaurants along Wells Street—Newspaper Row—to eat, drink coffee, and argue until the small hours of the morning. Then, as now, a newspaperman could get tickets to whatever plays or shows were in town. Bert, determined not to miss anything, saw them all: opera at the grand old Auditorium, with Tetrazzini and other great singers, olio and vaudeville, Shakespeare, musical comedy, ballet.

Bert went everywhere, knew everybody, from the grand moguls of Chicago society to the gaudy denizens of the Levee. His persuasive tongue helped him gain entree to places where reporters were normally barred. It wasn't long before he graduated to the status of a full-fledged feature writer, with his articles syndicated by Hearst from coast to coast.

One night an ad in the paper caught his eye. The Great Gypsy Troupe of dancers was appearing in a Loop theater, and everyone was singing their praises. Well, now, Bert thought, I've nothing to do tonight, and watching the Great Gypsy Troupe sounds like a good way to do it. It was no trick at all to persuade the city desk to give him a ticket—no self-respecting reporter ever paid for a ticket to a theater—and 8:30 that evening found Bert sitting front row, center, watching the dancers. After a little while it occurred to him that he was watching only one dancer: a lovely, slim girl with black hair and eyes, whose movements were unusually graceful.

Now there, he said to himself, is a thing to see!

For the rest of the evening, as far as Bert Lennon was concerned, there was only one dancer on the stage. His eyes followed her admiringly. Was she returning his ardent gaze? He smiled, and there was no doubt of it—her lovely mouth returned his smile.

"I'll go meet her after the show," he said. "Ah, no, that would be a foolish thing. Let me come back here tomorrow night, in the same seat, and see if she will smile at me again."

Next day it was hard for Bert to keep his mind on an interview with the police commissioner and an article on the importance of the city as a seaport for foreign trade. Between his eyes and the typewriter he kept seeing the pretty face framed in dark hair.

At noon he went, as was his habit often, to Old St. Peter's Roman Catholic Church, just south of the Loop, to pay a visit. Old St. Peter's was a favorite of newspapermen. He knelt for a short while near the rear. In the dim shadows ahead, a woman knelt, her head bowed. When she raised her head, Bert's heart leaped—it was the girl he already thought of as his—the little gypsy dancer!

She arose to leave and he followed. Outside, he said, "Ah—Miss——"

His usual blarney seemed to have deserted him. She turned and stared frostily. "I—ah—excuse me," Bert stammered, "I just wanted to say I saw you dance last night and you were wonderful!"

Her frostiness melted and she smiled a little. "*Danke* —thank you! *Ja*, I see you there *mit*—with the red hair."

Her voice was just as Bert had known it would be, low-pitched and bewitching. For a minute he stood, smiling foolishly, and she turned to go.

"Wait," he said. "I'm coming again to see you tonight.

My name is Bert Lennon. I just dropped into the church, and saw you, and thought I'd say hello."

"Hello," she said gravely, bowed slightly, and again turned to go. He fell into step beside her.

"You haven't told me your name," he said, giving her his best smile.

She laughed. "*Ach*, so—so bold, you Americans! My name is Barbara Heinrich, I am dancer, and now I must go, eh?"

Bert's self-confidence had come back. He took Barbara's arm. "Fine," he said. "I'll walk right along with you. I know a nice little place where we can have lunch."

"Lunch?" she said doubtfully. "What is?"

Bert had eaten in enough German restaurants to know. "Lunch," he said, making a wide gesture. "*Mittagessen. Kartoffelsalad*, Miss Heinrich. *Bratwurst mit—mit* something or other."

She laughed, delightfully, and they were friends. "I do not think wise," she said. "But I go. You tell me words, eh?"

The lunch stretched until late afternoon, while Bert's editor scorched the telephone looking for him. Bert didn't even mind the bawling out he got when he finally showed up at the office. He hardly heard it—he was thinking of a beautiful girl with black hair, a throaty laugh, and a wonderful way of pronouncing English words.

They met again next day, and the next, and every evening Bert was in the same seat at the theater. Each night her smile, for him alone, grew warmer. So engrossed was Bert that he didn't notice the black looks that were com-

46034

ing his way from other members of the Great Gypsy Troupe.

In their all-too-brief meetings, Barbara told him about her life. It sounded strange and exciting to him. She had been born in Germany, had been sent as a small girl to Russia where she had studied ballet in the great school at Moscow, and then had lived and worked in Budapest, in the Austro-Hungarian Empire.

"I am not gypsy," she said. "I am *echte Deutsche*—a real German. There are gypsies in the troupe, though, Bert." A frown wrinkled her forehead. "Janos and Miklos. *Ach*, they are the bad ones!"

Bert didn't understand. "Bad? Why?"

But Barbara wouldn't tell him. That night at the ballet, he looked for Janos and Miklos. With a shock, he realized that two of the male dancers were scowling ferociously at him over the footlights. What was the matter with them? he wondered.

Bert got another shock after the performance, as he waited at the stage door for Barbara. The doorman handed him an envelope with a note. "For the big redheaded fella," he said. "That must be you."

The note was from Barbara:

Liebling, is better you not to see me more. We leave Chicago soon and you forget me. Believe me, better so. Barbara.

Stunned, Bert brushed aside the doorman and ran into the backstage area of the theater. Groups of chattering dancers were coming out. Stopping one girl, he asked: "Miss Heinrich—Fräulein Heinrich. Where is she?"

"Barbie?" said the gypsy girl. "She's in that room, Red."

Even in his bewilderment Bert grinned a little. There was a New Yorker if ever he'd heard one! He knocked on Barbara's door, and her voice said, "*Wer ist's*—who is, please?"

"Bert. Barbara, let me in."

She opened the door. He could see that she'd been crying. "*Ach*, Bert, *liebling*, not tonight should you come!" She let him in.

"Barbara—sweetheart—what's the matter? What does this note mean?"

Hesitantly, she told him. Miklos and Janos were both in love with her. They were bitter rivals of each other, but when another man came along they had banded together in their hatred of him. They were bad—bad! she repeated. They had told her that if she didn't stop seeing Bert, they would beat him up.

Bert laughed. "Is that all! Why, acushla, do you think an Irishman is scared of a couple of gypsy dancers?" He looked at her. "Do you love them—either of them?"

"No—oh, no!"

He came closer and took her in his arms. "Do you love somebody else?"

The dark head drooped lower until it was against his shoulder.

"Me?" he said softly. She nodded. That was all he needed. "Ha!" he shouted triumphantly. "She loves me!" He went on more quietly, "Listen, *mo roisin dhu*—that's Irish for 'my little dark rose,' Barbara—if you love me, there's not anybody going to keep us apart. Not anybody! Now you take my arm and we'll walk out of here, and if

53

Miklos or Janos or anybody else tries anything, why . . ."
He clenched his big fists.

She smiled, tremulously, and took his arm. Together
they went out of the theater into the dark alley which led
to Jackson Boulevard.

And there, looming up darkly against the light, were
two figures. Janos and Miklos.

"Get behind me," Bert told Barbara. He went forward.

The two dancers came to meet him, slightly separated,
moving gracefully and silently.

"Now," Bert said in commanding tones, "I am taking
my wife-to-be, and we are going from this place. And I
would not like to be the man who tried to stop me!"

When he was angry, County Cork echoed more plainly
in his voice.

One of the dancers said something in a foreign tongue.
The other snarled, "You have your women, leave ours
alone!"

"Now, hold on!" Bert said, raising a commanding
hand. "I think maybe you boys have the wrong idea. I
don't——"

Janos broke in passionately. "Ideas! I know what is with
you! You see dancing girl, right away you think no good,
eh? Right away you send flowers, send candy, have fun
with poor dancing girl! Is no good, no good! We take care
our women, we——" He lapsed into a torrent of Hungarian.

"Ah!" Bert said softly. "I see. Well, look you now,
Janos—or is it Miklos?—I don't blame you for wanting to
take care of your women. But I'm not having fun with a

poor dancing girl, as you say. Why, heaven bless you, lad, I want to marry her!"

"That's right," Barbara said tremulously. "Marry!" She hugged Bert's arm and looked up at him with adoring eyes.

The two gypsies looked at each other, and held a short conversation in Hungarian. Bert, sensing their doubt, said:

"We're in love. I don't care whether she's a dancer or the daughter of the Earl of Cork, she's the girl I want. I'll be friends if you want, my boys, but if not——"

"Earl of Cork?" Janos said doubtfully, and turned to Barbara. "You want marry this—this red man, little one?"

"*Ja!*" she breathed. "I love him!"

The two gypsies held a hurried conversation, then Janos shrugged. "Marry, that is different, eh? We think— plenty times, people try take our women—you un'erstan'?"

"Sure," Bert said quickly. "I understand."

"That no good, eh? Well, you are brave, Irishman. If you marry Barbara, you good to her—we let you have her."

"You'll *let* me have her!" Bert shouted. "Why——" Suddenly he began to laugh. To be arguing here, in a dark alley, with two dancers who were only anxious that their adored Barbara wouldn't be led astray, suddenly seemed to him ridiculous. Why, Janos and Miklos weren't such bad fellows after all!

Miklos, puzzled, said something. Janos answered; then they, too, began to laugh. Finally, Barbara joined in. The four of them stood there, laughing.

"I'll take good care of her," Bert promised. "Don't worry."

He held out his hand. Miklos shook it, then Janos.

They began laughing again, and a policeman peered into the alley. "Now thin, what's all this?" he asked, with a thick brogue.

Bert put on an even thicker one. "Why, a happy day entirely, it is. I've just offered me hand, and it's taken in love by the colleen here, and we're after celebratin' a bit."

"Good, thin!" said the policeman, pleased. "Luck to ye, big man!"

The four of them walked down the street together. They walked along Michigan Avenue, while Miklos and Janos sang old gypsy songs, and Barbara lent her voice to an old German *lied*, and Bert contributed some of the Irish songs his mother had taught him.

One of them was an old nonsense song that he had sung when he was very young:

"Knick knack, paddy whack, give the dog a bone . . ."

Bert didn't have the second sight, granted to some by the sidhe—the fairy people—or he would have seen that fifty years from then, four of his granddaughters would be singing that same old song together, while millions listened.

But it was a wonderful courtship, and a grand wedding to follow, and life was good, indeed, to a young fellow who had found his love.

CHAPTER IV

No Greater Love

Bert Lennon and Barbara Heinrich were married January 13, 1910, in St. Paul's Cathedral, St. Paul, Minnesota, where Bert had taken a job as a feature writer with the St. Paul *Pioneer Press*. The Reverend J. J. Lawler, pastor, performed the ceremony, and James Delancy and Mrs. Emma O'Leary were the best man and bridesmaid. For twenty-two years Bert and Barbara had a happy, productive life.

After four years in St. Paul, they returned to Chicago. When they moved from Chicago to southern California in 1917 they were already the parents of three sons: Jack, born in St. Paul in 1911; Jim, born in St. Paul in 1913; and Bill, born in Chicago in 1915.

Bert Lennon never lost the joy of living which he had when he was young. He became a well-known newspaper syndicate writer and later worked as a publicist for Thomas H. Ince, movie producer, and the Metro-Goldwyn-Mayer Studios. His seven sons and one daughter remember him as a man who was usually smiling, and was likely to lift his voice in song at any time. Their childhood seemed full of music. Bert had a vast store of songs, Irish and American, and never could go for long without breaking into one of them in his rich baritone. Barbara, too, had music bred into her; her songs were from Germany or Russia or Hungary.

Small wonder that their children grew up with music as much a part of their lives as eating!

After they moved to Venice, near Los Angeles, the Lennon family kept growing. Tom was born in 1916; Bob in 1918; Ted in 1920; Pat in 1925; and the baby of the family, their idolized only daughter, Mary, in 1928.

It should be remarked here that all of the seven boys and one girl are doing well. Jack is the First Secretary in the U. S. Embassy in Pakistan; he is married and has two children. Jim is a sports announcer in Santa Monica, California, and has other TV shows; he is married and has five children. Bill, of course, we know. Tom lives in Garden Grove, California, with his wife and two children, and is an executive at Douglas Aircraft Corporation. Bob also works at Douglas Aircraft as a chief inspector. He, his wife, and six children live in Venice. Ted works for Lawrence Welk; like Bill, he lives in Venice, is married and the father of eleven children. Pat is in the contracting business, and lives in Venice with his wife and five children. Mary—Mrs. Don Blaser—and her husband and five children live in Venice, where Mr. Blaser works for a wholesale meat company.

It is in Bill that our chief interest centers.

All the older boys were musical, but Bill seemed to have inherited more of a feeling for music than any of the others. When the boys were little, Barbara Lennon, like all mothers, sang them to sleep with lullabies. Sometimes they were old songs of Germany or Ireland; sometimes they were new songs of America; sometimes they were sacred songs.

When Bill was only two years old, he startled his mother by humming the tune of the lullaby along with her—humming it perfectly. A year later Barbara got another surprise. As she was working in the kitchen, she heard a clear, childish voice singing a song she loved, a song about the Virgin Mary: "Mother Dearest, Mother Fairest." Quietly, she followed the sound. It was little Billy, playing happily by himself and singing.

She could hardly wait until her husband Bert came home. When he did she told him to sit quietly, and turned to Billy. "Honey, do you remember that song you were singing today?"

The little boy nodded solemnly.

"Could you sing it for Daddy?"

Without another word, Billy lifted his head and sang. When he had finished, his father swung him up in the air. "Ah, that was fine, Billy! Why, what a songbird we have here!" Barbara looked on, tears of happiness in her eyes.

For the next six months, Billy and his brother Jimmy, who was two years older, were the singers in the family. At parties, at Christmas and Easter, and often just for their parents, they sang the old airs their mother and father loved.

When Bill was about three and a half years of age, he fell seriously ill. Doctors diagnosed his condition as a pinched nerve and he was put to bed. As the weeks and months passed, Billy became more and more listless. His father tried in every way to cheer him up and bring back his smile. Once he brought Billy a live white rabbit, but Billy took one look at the rabbit and turned his head away. His father left the room hurriedly, tears rolling down his cheeks. Later, he said he would have given anything if only Billy had smiled.

After a year and a half in bed, Billy improved. At the age of five he was obliged to learn to walk all over again. His cheery disposition returned, and to his parents' happiness he began to sing again.

In 1923 the new parish of St. Mark's was formed in Venice, the first Mass being celebrated in an old dance hall. When Billy was twelve, he joined the choir and was soon its outstanding member. The boy sang naturally and unaffectedly, without "showing off" and without any false reluctance. To him singing came as easily as breathing.

When Billy was fourteen years old, his father took him to St. Mary's school to entertain the children. Mrs. Ethel Boswell, his accompanist, went along. The auditorium on the second floor of the school building was filled to overflowing. Many of the younger boys were obliged to stand on the balcony outside the auditorium and watch the performance through the windows. While Billy was singing his first song, he saw the boys on the balcony making faces at him. They grimaced and went through motions indicating they were making fun of him.

In the middle of his second song he stopped abruptly, left the stage, ran down the corridor onto the balcony, and started swinging right and left.

It had happened so suddenly, it took a little while before his father could get to Billy and grab him, but not before he had pounded several boys. His shirt was torn, his pants ruined. This unscheduled entertainment ended the assembly.

Mrs. Boswell, very much embarrassed, said sternly on the way home, "Bert, when we reach home you give Billy the beating of his life. My goodness! I was never so humiliated! Whatever possessed you to do that, Billy?"

Arriving home, Mr. Lennon, who had been failing in health and now used a cane, took Billy upstairs and then broke out laughing. He said, "Billy boy, that was funny! I never knew you had it in you!" After enjoying a good laugh, he said, "Now, while I beat the wall with my cane, you yell so those downstairs will think you are getting a beating!"

The incident didn't spoil Billy's singing career. The Reverend W. J. Stewart, pastor of St. Mark's, recognizing a rare talent, had Billy sing a solo at each Mass. One Sunday a rather bulkily built man with a wide, engaging smile came into St. Mark's for Mass. When he heard the pure, clear tenor floating down from the choir loft, his head jerked erect and his eyes widened. What was this? Such a voice, in an out-of-the-way church?

After Mass, the man called on Father Stewart. He presented his card. He was Tito Schipa, world-renowned tenor, operatic star, who had been hailed in all the great cities of Europe and the Americas. Schipa was then thirty-eight years old, at the height of his career.

"I must meet this boy," he told Father Stewart. "Rarely have I heard such a voice! Untrained, yes, but purest gold!"

That was the beginning for Billy. Things happened

fast. Schipa invited the boy to his home, and at a private audition Billy sang for him.

The great tenor put his arm around Billy's shoulders. "My boy, you have great talent. It must not be wasted. You will work, eh? And I will help."

Schipa let it be known that Billy was his protégé. The boy sang at the christening party of Schipa's daughter, Liana, while such greats of the film world as Douglas Fairbanks and Mary Pickford listened and approved. The Reverend Nicholas Connolly of St. Monica's Church, Santa Monica, invited Billy to appear as a soloist, and his songs were heard by the beloved Irish concert tenor, John McCormack. McCormack invited Billy and his father to his home and during the visit, Billy sang the beautiful ballad, "Believe Me, If All Those Endearing Young Charms." Everyone who heard him praised Billy's singing. He still keeps a thick scrapbook, stuffed with notes of appreciation from groups before which he appeared, "rave notices" by newspaper music critics, and programs where his name headed the list. The critics used such phrases as "a real artist . . . pure phrasing, faultless tone . . . a voice to wring your heart." In 1929 the University of Southern California's Music Department acclaimed Billy as one of four outstanding young musicians in the United States. He sang a song especially for President Herbert Hoover; it was recorded, with a piano accompaniment by Carrie Jacobs Bond, famous composer of such loved songs as "The End of a Perfect Day." Madame Ernestine Schumann-Heink, one of the greatest contraltos of all time, spoke gracious words of introduction on the recording. In return, the President sent a letter of thanks to Master Lennon for his singing.

Billy sang in theaters up and down the West Coast, on the Keith-Orpheum and the Fanchon and Marco circuits, sometimes as many as thirty-one performances each week. In 1929, 1930, and 1931 he was the featured artist at the Easter Sunrise Services at Hollywood Bowl, an event which attracts more than a hundred thousand people yearly. He also held three of his own concerts there.

He and his three brothers appeared as a quartet with Paul Whiteman's Band. Whiteman, "the King of Jazz," had the most outstanding popular orchestra at that time. Billy made numerous appearances on radio; hundreds of thousands heard him.

It was a wonderful time, a magical time, for a young boy. And then, in 1931, it all ended suddenly and tragically.

With all this activity, Billy kept his family ties close. He and his six brothers and sister remember, affectionately, musical evenings at home, when they sang together or by themselves until long after they should have been asleep.

In particular, Bill remembers his father winding up those wonderful evenings of song with one of his favorites, "Sing Me to Sleep":

> *"Sing me to sleep, the shadows fall;*
> *Let me forget the world and all."*

Herbert Lennon had been in poor health for four years, and the shadows fell for him at the early age of forty-five.

The lean and now frail man, whose flaming hair had faded a little but whose voice was as booming as ever, died suddenly, leaving a widow with eight children to support.

There was no time to give way to grief. Barbara Lennon was tiny—only 105 pounds—but determined. She had never let hardship defeat her and she wasn't going to start now. With the help of prayer and boundless faith, she knew she could meet the challenge.

Meet it she did, although it was a hard struggle. In 1931 the Great Depression held the world in its grip. Money was hard to come by and jobs were hard to find. Jack, the eldest, postponed his marriage for a year to help support the family.

For Billy, it meant the end—for a while at least—of his musical ambition. Singing was too precarious a way of earning a living. Besides, his heart wasn't in it any more. Bill hadn't lost his interest in music, but without his father, who had always been his friend, adviser, and coach, things just weren't the same. Besides, he had to pitch in and help. He was nearly seventeen, almost a man, and he wanted to contribute his part. After graduation from high school, Bill got a job which paid him $10 a week. Ten dollars meant a lot more in 1934 than it does now. Billy turned over the $10 to his mother, who kept $9 and gave him 50 cents' spending money and an I.O.U. for another 50 cents.

Still, even with everyone helping, it was a hard fight. The boys put aside their male dignity and cheerfully helped with housework and taking care of their baby sister Mary, who was only three. Sometimes the only thing they had to eat for dinner was cornmeal patties and gravy.

Several times well-meaning officials of the California Welfare Department notified Mrs. Lennon that they would have to break up her family. Of course, they got nowhere. She replied bristling with defiance:

"Maybe we don't always eat like kings, but none of my children ever went hungry yet! And maybe our clothes aren't in the latest fashion, but they are clean and neat! Besides, anything we may lack in luxuries we more than make up for in living together as a family, and nobody, nobody at all, is going to break us up!"

That was that. Wisely, the California welfare authorities retreated.

From his mother, Bill recalls, he learned a lesson he has never forgotten. One Saturday night he picked up his hard-earned salary of $10 and started home but on the way decided to stop by for his friend who worked at a place where bingo or lotto was played. While waiting for the other boy, he decided to buy a few cards and play the game in hopes he could increase his $10 to $20 or more. Bill knew he shouldn't—but wouldn't it be wonderful if he could take home a pocketful of money? The Lennons hadn't seen much money since Dad had died.

His $10 shrank to $5 in a short time. Then he won, and won again. Now he had $15 and was beginning to think of himself as lucky. He took several cards, and before he knew what had happened, his $15 was 8, 6, 2— and then he had only 25 cents left!

Sick, ashamed, and hating himself, Bill wandered the streets, not wanting to face his mother. That money could have bought food for almost a week! It could have bought poor little Mary the shoes she needed, or—or—a dozen things! Until four in the morning he walked aimlessly. Finally, he squared his shoulders. Better face it. It was cowardly to run away and that's what he was doing.

His mother met him at the door, her face drawn with worry. "Where have you been, Bill?" she asked quietly.

Shamefaced, he told her everything, not sparing himself. Then he stood with his head down, waiting for the anger he knew he deserved. But Barbara Lennon was wise enough to know that he had learned his lesson, that a tongue-lashing would do no good. She only said:

"Billy boy, you will never know what this means to me."

She turned away, leaving him to lie awake the rest of the night, thinking about what he had done. How could he have hurt his mother so! Never would he forget the sadness in her eyes.

He never did forget—and he was never again tempted to throw away his money.

Gradually, things got better. The older boys had good jobs, and the days of cornmeal patties were behind them. Still, there was little money to spend on amusements. This was no hardship. As the Lennons always had, they made their own entertainment. Bill's voice was still a fine one, and he and his brothers formed a quartet. They all shared in musical talent.

It wasn't long before the Lennon brothers—Bill, Jim, Pat, and Ted—were in demand for parties and concerts. Bob later replaced Jim in the quartet, after Jim took a night job as a fight announcer.

The quartet kept going. Their names began to appear

on programs. They were heard over radio and television. Perhaps, if they had kept singing together, they would have become as famous as Bill's daughters were to become. But it was not to be. Show business was still too precarious, and there were wives, Mother, and the little ones to think of.

The quartet kept active for a long time, but less and less as a source of income and more and more for pure pleasure. The brothers still sing together and still get a lot of fun out of it, but rarely are they heard by any audience except their own families.

In 1935 a chance meeting changed Bill's life. He and his friend John Wright went to see their old alma mater, Venice High, play football against University High School in West Los Angeles. It was a good, tight game, and for the first half Bill followed the plays closely, cheering for Venice.

Just before the gun went off to end the half, he looked around. A few rows behind him sat a girl he knew, Afton Conger. With her was a girl he hadn't seen before, a stunning brunet. Her curling black hair hung to her shoulders, and her pretty face was alive with mischief and vivacity.

Just as his father had twenty-five years earlier, Bill told himself: There's a girl I must meet!

At the half, Afton and her friend went to buy an ice cream bar. Bill touched John's arm. "I suddenly feel the need of an ice cream bar," he said. "Come on!"

Afton waved and smiled, "Hi, Bill—John."

"Hi, Afton," Bill said. She noticed the direction his glance was taking and laughed.

"I want you to meet a friend of mine, Isabelle Denning," Afton said.

The brown eyes smiled into his, the clasp of her hand was warm and firm. "I'm glad to know you," Isabelle said.

"And I'm glad to know *you*, Isabelle," Bill said.

He wasted no time. The next night he called Isabelle to ask for a date. She agreed. They had a wonderful evening together. It was only the first of many. Both of them knew, right away, that this was something special. They were still too young to think of getting married, but it wasn't long before friendship became love. Both knew they would marry, someday.

Isabelle was a native of Los Angeles. She, her mother, and brother Dan had recently moved to Venice. Isabelle's mother, born Ysabelle Alvarez, was of Spanish descent, born in San Diego in 1892. She had married Danford Denning, from Missouri, of Irish descent, in 1915. Denning, too, was in show business. He was a song-and-dance man, who traveled around the country to appear on vaudeville programs. The Depression had hit him too. Besides, vaudeville was dying. Denning knew no other way of making a livelihood, while jobs were getting scarcer all the time. Mrs. Denning had to take a job to keep her little family together. She was a chocolate dipper, working in one factory after another, forced to move frequently. Isabelle and her brother Dan had to change schools thirty-eight times and lived in fifty-four different homes!

Bill's mother liked Isabelle, and when, three years after

they had met, Bill announced they were going to be married, Mrs. Lennon approved. She told Bill:

"I'm glad. Isabelle is a wonderful girl. But Bill, just one thing bothers me. Isabelle doesn't seem to belong to any church."

Bill nodded. "I know. We've talked about that many times, Mother. She feels the lack of a church, and we've come to a conclusion."

"What's that, son?"

"Isabelle has decided to become a Catholic. I didn't try to persuade her, Mom. It's her own idea. She's taking instructions three times a week." He smiled. "Just to show you how much in earnest she is, she has to miss her dinner on the nights she attends her religion class."

Barbara Lennon laughed. "That shows a fine spirit!" She kissed Bill. "That answers my question, son. I know you'll be happy!"

Happy they were. Bill and Isabelle were married February 19, 1939, in St. Mark's, where Bill had sung as a boy. The young couple set up housekeeping in a small home near his mother's, in Venice. Isabelle gave up her job as a dentist's assistant to devote all her time to her husband and her home.

That same year, December 1, their first baby was born: a blue-eyed, lovely girl who was christened Dianne Barbara.

The second baby, another girl, came in April 1941. She had the dark hair and eyes of her mother's mother. She was named Margaret Anne. The third daughter was another brunet, Kathleen Mary, who arrived August 2,

1943, and on June 15, 1946, another blue-eyed blonde, Janet Elizabeth, was born.

The house was already too small. It was filled to every corner with childish shouts, laughter and, of course, singing. But the children kept coming, each one welcomed joyfully: February 8, 1950, Danny, with blue eyes and brown hair; November 9, 1951, another son, Patrick, as blond as Dianne; on March 5, 1953, Mary; on July 29, 1954, Billy; on October 16, 1955, Mimi; on May 9, 1957, Joseph; and on January 24, 1959, their eleventh child, another lovely little dark-haired girl, Anne Madeline. Joseph and Anne arrived after the Lennons had moved into their present home.

Wonderful years, filled with the joy of living and giving. Bill had left Douglas Aircraft for another job which provided more money for his growing family. After a few years with a sporting goods store and Pepsi-Cola, he got a job with the Edgemar Dairy Company. The hours were long, but the pay was good. He was a happy man. With a family like that, how could he not be happy?

Now it's time to go back for a closer look at the childhood of Dianne (DeeDee), Margaret Anne (Peggy), Kathleen Mary (Kathy) and Janet (Janny).

CHAPTER V

Reading, 'Riting and 'Rithmetic

Fall, 1945! A fateful and dramatic year was drawing to a close. So many things had happened! President Roosevelt had died. The Germany of Hitler and his Nazis had been defeated. Atomic bombs had exploded over Hiroshima and Nagasaki, and the shattered Japanese Empire had surrendered. A group of statesmen were meeting in San Francisco to forge, they hoped, a new organization of United Nations which would forever end such terrible wars as the one which had just been won.

All over the world, all over the United States, people were uttering prayers of thanksgiving that the great war had ended. Mothers and fathers were turning their attention to their own little problems and the business of raising their families.

So it was with the Lennons. That September they were to mark an important event: their daughter Dianne was starting in first grade.

Everyone who has sent the eldest child of a family off to school for the first time can remember what an important day it is. The child is the center of attention and realizes it. So it was with Dianne. In her five-year-old way, she realized that "going to school" meant the beginning of a new life. From now on, she would be marching off to school every day, just as Daddy went to work.

One night Sis Lennon heard Dianne sobbing bitterly in her bed, while her younger sisters lay asleep. "What's the matter, honey?" Mrs. Lennon asked softly, putting her arm around the little girl's shoulders.

"Oh, Mommy," Dianne whispered, "I've been thinking. After I go to school, I won't be your little girl any more! Peggy will be!"

"Hush, now, and don't be silly," Sis told her. "Of course you'll be my little girl. Just because you're going to school doesn't make any difference."

"But I'm nearly six years old!" Dianne sobbed. "I'm not a little girl any more!"

Sis Lennon couldn't help laughing, but managed to soothe Dianne's injured feelings by assuring her that the mere fact of her attending first grade wouldn't age her overnight.

"And can I still play with dolls, and everything?" Dianne asked, only half convinced. Finally, reassured, she sank back and slept.

Her bruised feelings were further helped by the wonderful new blue dress her mother was making for her. Mrs. Lennon made most of the girls' clothes; she is adept at designing and needlework. Besides, the long years of near poverty had taught her the lesson of thrift. In 1945, times were good. The Depression had long since become only a memory, and Bill's job brought in enough money for them to live comfortably. Nonetheless, feeding and

DIANNE

PEGGY

KATHY

JANET

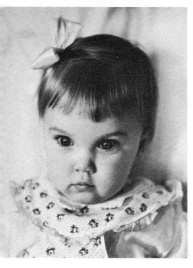

DIANNE

PEGGY

The Lennon sisters at an early age

KATHY

JANET

First a duo:
Peggy and Dianne

Then a trio:
Peggy, Dianne, and
Kathy

The quartet is ready:
Kathy, Dianne, Janet,
and Peggy

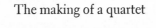

The making of a quartet

The favorites of millions

Where the Lennon family used to live

The present Lennon home

The Lennon family. Left to right, front row: Billy, Danny, Pat. Left to right, back row: Kathy, Peggy, Mrs. Isabelle Lennon holding baby Joey, Mr. William Lennon, Dianne holding Mimi, and Janet.

clothing a large family is an expensive business, and Sis knew how to make every nickel count.

Peggy and Kathy watched with wide, envious eyes as their mother fitted the new dress on Dianne. "Never mind," Dianne said consolingly. "After a while you'll be big girls, too, and you can have a blue dress. Or maybe," she added, struck by a sudden thought, "Peggy can have this one next year and I can get another new one."

Peggy restrained her enthusiasm at this proposal, and Sis said that of course each of her girls would get a new dress for school.

Finally the great day came. Dianne faced it with another outburst of tears. "I don't want to go away! I want to stay home and play with Peggy and Kathy and Freckles!"

Freckles, the blond cocker, put up his nose and wailed, understanding that something was going on. Peggy and Kathy, torn between delight in having a sister big enough to go to school and woe at losing a playmate, clung together and howled.

Finally Sis, holding firmly to Dianne's hand, managed to get her out of the house and walking down the street. Dianne, turning to wave at her sisters who stood at the window, seemed to have forgotten her tears in the excitement of going to school.

"Peggy and Kathy are good girls," she told her mother in an important, woman-of-the-world tone. "But they're still pretty little."

"Yes, honey," Sis said. "They're not big, like you."

Since St. Mark's parish did not yet have its own school, Dianne was enrolled at Theodore Roosevelt Public School about five blocks from their home. When they arrived, Dianne had fully recovered her self-possession. Entranced by the delights of the big first grade room, the tiny chairs and playthings, she immediately began to make friends with her classmates. When the time came to say good-by to her mother, Dianne announced that she liked school and—after some doubt—had made up her mind to stay.

On her way home, Sis felt foolish tears forming against her eyelids. I'm as bad as the little girls are, she told herself impatiently. But she did feel as if, somehow, a milestone in their lives had been reached and passed. Every parent knows the feeling—their baby is growing up!

Dianne came back in a few hours, bulging with stories of what they did and how one girl cried and cried— "Wasn't she bad?"—and a little boy had stuck his tongue out at her. Next morning, though, Dianne again displayed a marked reluctance to go to school. It wasn't until two weeks had passed that she accepted the routine of hurrying off to school, while her little sisters could dawdle over their oatmeal.

Two weeks after school started, Freckles the cocker decided to enroll too. Dianne was late getting up that morning, and had to run part of the way. It wasn't until she saw the children pointing and heard their giggles that she realized Freckles had come along. The dog, excited and pleased over the prospect of a whole roomful of children to play with, wriggled and wagged his tail.

"Dianne," the teacher, Mrs. Smith, said, "you know you can't bring a dog into school!"

"I didn't know he was following me," Dianne said.

The children giggled, and one said, "Mary had a little lamb . . ."

"Well," Mrs. Smith said firmly, "he'll just have to go." She spread her arms and advanced on Freckles. "Shoo! Outside!"

Freckles was delighted. This was going to be a grand game! He scampered under the chairs, with the teacher in pursuit. The children joined in gleefully, with squeals and shouts. "There he goes! Oh, my, he's going to knock over the fern! Get him, get him!" They jumped up and led a mad chase around the room, while Freckles barked frantically. In a few minutes it occurred to the teacher that nothing was being accomplished except a lot of noise, and she told Dianne to corral Freckles. The dog came obediently. Dianne picked him up and put him outside, and the classroom finally settled down.

(Even now, Dianne occasionally meets people with whom she went to first grade. Almost invariably they say, "Remember the time your dog got loose?")

Freckles' escapade was the high point of the academic year. It went quickly enough, although Dianne was a little disappointed she was not reading and writing fluently when the summer vacation was ushered in by June. However, as her mother explained, those accomplishments would come in good time.

Two years later, in September 1947, it was Peggy's turn. For weeks ahead of time, Dianne fortified her with sage advice about school and with enthralling tales of the scholarly life. As a result, when her turn came to kiss the family good-by and start off for school, Peggy went eagerly. Her teacher, Mrs. Nuhard, remembers Peggy as an excellent pupil. This left poor little Kathy at home, longing for the time when she, too, would be important enough to go to school. Every day, long before her adored older sisters were due home, Kathy had her nose pressed to the window, watching for them.

When they did come, and the three girls were together again, there were still hours of sunshine before dinner. In southern California, people spend most of their time out of doors.

Dianne was the outdoor type. Not a tomboy, she still loved running and jumping. Whenever Sis Lennon looked out the window, she could usually see Dianne's blond hair flying as she raced after a high fly ball or rounded third base on her way home.

Peggy's tastes were quieter. She liked dolls and toys and would sit by the hour with her doll family, making up long stories about their lives. Peggy's dolls, in common with most other dolls, led a troubled existence; they got sick as often as people in radio soap operas, and Peggy spent a good deal of her time making them well.

Kathy was still too little to be much of a baseball player. But there were plenty of games all three could play together: hopscotch, jacks, skipping rope—all the games girls have played for centuries.

Sometimes Bill Lennon played with them. Not as often as he would have liked, because his hours were long and his job tiring. But whenever he could, he and the girls got up a game of baseball, or some other game of their own devising.

It was a happy time, a happy household. As far as any

of them knew, or hoped, they would continue living just as they had been doing. They liked their life—work, school, church, play. They liked Venice. It was neither the swankiest nor the wealthiest of the hundreds of towns around Los Angeles, but it was their home town and it suited them. There they would stay. The years passed quickly, each bringing its own memories to treasure. In 1947 Dianne passed another milestone—her First Communion. The Lennons made this happy occasion the opportunity for a big family get-together. Uncles, aunts, cousins, grandparents, all converged on the little house in Venice for a day of rejoicing. It was a real old-fashioned family party, with a big dinner, games for the young ones, talk and reminiscing for their elders and, of course, a session of singing.

On June 15, 1946, another blue-eyed girl was born—Janet Elizabeth. Now the quartet was complete.

In 1949 the Lennon family marked two important events: Peggy made her First Communion in May, and in September Kathy started proudly to school. By that time, St. Mark's parish school had been completed and Kathy enrolled with Peggy in the new parochial school. Kathy's teacher's name was Sister Mary Felicitas.

Does all this sound as if the girls were little angels, never getting into trouble, never squabbling with one another, never coming into the house with muddy feet, or tearing their clothes, or playing tricks, as all other children do? If that's the idea you have—well, you're wrong. They were good girls, yes, and still are—but not goody-good girls, and there's a vast difference.

There were as many skinned knees, as many shouts of

"You did!" "I did not!" in the Lennon household as in any other comparable one. The girls did silly things and thoughtless ones; they were scolded and, when they needed it, spanked.

Peggy borrowed Dianne's new mittens without troubling to tell Dianne, and lost one. Dianne tore her dress, tried to sew it so her mother wouldn't see, made a botch of it and ran the needle under her fingernail in the bargain. Kathy hid a chocolate bar from her sisters, but unfortunately thought best to hide it under the cushion of a chair in the living room. When it was found three hot days later, it had melted, leaving a horrid mess which almost reduced Sis Lennon to tears.

Little things like that could be multiplied for pages, but what's the use? Exactly the same things happen in all families; that's part of living. The only place where children are always angelic, never cross or out of sorts, is between the pages of old-fashioned books like *Little Lord Fauntleroy* or *Elsie Dinsmore*. Nobody reads them any more. Nobody ever lived who was as good as Elsie Dinsmore was supposed to be. A good thing, too—Elsie, in the book, was a hopeless little prig.

Which is exactly what the Lennon girls are not. They have had their feuds and their disagreements, their fits of the sulks and temper, their floods of tears. The point is, though, that they have never been sneaky or mean or sly; they have never held a grudge and whenever one of them did something she knew was wrong, she was always immediately sorry for it.

Mischief, yes. A youngster who never gets into mischief isn't worth much!

Teasing, yes. The girl who never teased anyone is another character met only between the covers of dull old books. For instance:

When the time came for Kathy to make her First Communion—she'd been looking forward to it for a long time—she was ill. At St. Mark's the girls went one Sunday, the boys the next; and Kathy was the only girl among a whole battalion of dressed-up little boys. She marched up the aisle, dressed in white with a veil, beside a small boy in a black suit.

Parents of the Communion class and the other parishioners smiled. Kathy and the boy looked for all the world like a bridal pair. In her devotion, Kathy hardly noticed— until Dianne and Peggy began plaguing her afterward. They giggled, asked, "How's your husband, Kathy?" and sang "Here Comes the Bride" until poor Kathy's life was a torment and a burden.

(But after their mother explained how miserable they were making Kathy, the two girls were stricken with remorse. They pooled their resources to buy Kathy a present to show they were sorry. The merger produced capital enough to invest in a large Good Humor bar. Kathy forgave them.)

Meanwhile, another part of their education was progressing nicely. That was singing.

Since Dianne had been old enough to talk, she had been singing. This was natural enough. Bill's voice was as true and melodious as ever. Sis's voice, although it lacked the professional polish of her husband's, was warm and vibrant, and Grandpa Denning, with his years

of professional experience on the stage, had a vast reper-
tory of songs.

Everybody sang. Bill sang while he shaved, Sis while
she cooked. It was the natural thing to burst out in song
whenever the fancy took one of them, and the girls accepted it naturally.

When Dianne was old enough to help around the
house, she copied her mother, singing as she worked. So
did Peggy, and so did Kathy, each in her turn. So began
the custom of singing over the dinner dishes.

Nursery rhymes at first, then songs they heard on the
radio, or old favorites like "Down by the Old Mill Stream"
and dozens more, or catchy tunes from Grandpa's vaudeville days. The girls sang them one after another, while
little Janet listened, big-eyed, occasionally joining in for
a measure or two.

Bill Lennon discovered early that the girls had relative
pitch—that is, the ear of each of them was keen enough
to discern the right note and accurate enough to sing it.
Hit an "A" on the piano and they will sing the same
"A" right back at you, without faltering or groping. (This
is not the same as "perfect pitch," a rare gift. Ask someone with perfect pitch, if you can find one, to sing—for
example, A-flat above middle C. He will sing it right on
pitch; he can "hear" the note in his mind.)

They began experimenting with harmony, coached by
Bill and Grandpa. Pass the Lennon house almost any
time, and you would have heard someone inside singing.
Probably more than one.

So they passed through their childhood. Some little

brothers arrived: Danny on February 8, 1950, and Pat on November 9, 1951.

On March 5, 1953 the girls were delighted when their mother brought home a new baby sister. She was a lovely child and was christened with the name Mary.

It was around this new little sister that the greatest tragedy of the Lennon family was to center.

CHAPTER VI

Thy Will Be Done

By 1954 the trio over the dinner dishes was already a quartet. Little Janet, only eight, joined in with her treble— a childish voice, but as true as those of her older sisters. It was obvious to Bill and Sis Lennon that they had something far above the ordinary.

One evening they sat in the front room, relaxing for a few minutes, while the girls did the dishes. It was March. Little Mary, just a year old, sat in her play pen, busily hitting a rubber ball with a plastic doll. From the kitchen came the chatter of the four girls, mixed with the sound of water and clatter of dishes. The girls were talking about plans for the coming summer.

Outside, the rain drizzled. Occasionally a car swished by the house, its lights cutting a path through the misty dusk. Dianne said:

"I wish it would get warm enough to swim. It's silly having the biggest ocean in the world only a couple of blocks away and not being able to go in it."

Kathy giggled. "Well, you're swimming in the dishpan. That ought to hold you for a while."

"Remember last summer," Peggy said, "when that big wave caught me and turned me over and Daddy had to haul me out by one foot?"

"He said you weren't big enough and he'd have to throw you back. That was the day Janet found the little octopus and scared us with it."

"Afraid of an ol' octopus!" Janet said scornfully. "I'm gonna find a real big one. You can find all kinds of nice things by the sea."

That set them off. "By the sea . . ." Dianne sang.

"By the sea, by the beautiful sea . . ." her sisters joined in, and they were singing. "When each wave comes a-rol-ling in, you can duck or swim . . ."

Bill and Sis looked at each other and smiled.

> *"Floating backwards, or forwards, or up in the air,*
> *Ma is rich, Pa is rich, so what do we care?*
> *I'd like to be beside you, down beside the sea,*
> *Beside the seaside, by the beautiful sea!"*

Bill rubbed his chin thoughtfully. "You know, those kids are good. I wonder whether they shouldn't get a chance?"

"Do you mean to sing professionally?" Sis asked, and he nodded. "They haven't thought about it," Sis went on. "They talk about what they'll do when they grow up. I hear them all the time, you know, and not one of them has said a thing about singing."

"They don't think of singing in terms of entertainment," Bill said. "To them, it's as natural as breathing. It's a way of expressing their thoughts and feelings."

"I know. Janet's ambition right now is to be a big-league ball player." She laughed. "She may make it, at that. Janet usually gets what she sets her mind to. Think of our Janet, the first girl to make the major leagues!"

"I have a hunch she'll outgrow wanting to be the world's greatest shortstop," Bill said.

"All I want for them is to be happy," Sis said. "It doesn't make any difference if they make a lot of money, or have their names up in lights. It's just——"

"I wasn't thinking of a lot of money or names up in lights. My idea was that since they like to sing, and they're so good at it, maybe they'd like to think about doing it professionally."

Sis nodded. "Well, you know the church is having a musical program in May. I'm sure Monsignor North would like them to sing. It might be good experience for them. If they liked it, and if the audience liked them, there might be other opportunities."

"We'll see. Yes, I think they should sing at St. Mark's." Bill let his thoughts drift backward down the years. "The entertainment business isn't easy, Sis. You know that—your father was in it so long. And I know it too—it's a tough grind!" He got up from his chair. From the kitchen came some weird sounds. Dianne and Janny were singing "Three Blind Mice," and the other two, for some reason, were singing "Row, Row, Row Your Boat." The results were astonishing. "Hey, you kids!" Bill called. "Let's get together on something!"

There was a sound of giggling, and the quartet compromised on "Among My Souvenirs," a tremendous improvement.

"Well, there's no hurry in deciding," Sis said. "They're only kids, after all, even Dianne. We don't want to make up their minds for them, or push them into anything."

Bill agreed. "Absolutely not. Guide them, yes, but don't drive them."

The three oldest girls did sing at St. Mark's musical in Culver City. Bill and Sis decided that Janet was too young for such a late evening, but yielded to her pleading and let her come along to watch.

A large audience was listening, but it didn't bother the girls. They were self-possessed, unafflicted by stage fright, sure of themselves. And the audience loved it. Bill and Sis, sitting unobtrusively in the auditorium, listened to the delighted comments of others nearby who didn't know, of course, that they were the parents of the three pretty girls on the stage.

"They're just like professionals!" one woman said. Her companion remarked, "Well, maybe they are." "Oh, no! Why, I've seen them for years in church. They're the Lennon girls."

They did have a professional air, Bill thought. They possessed that intangible something known as "stage presence." It's hard to describe, but it's easy to tell whether a performer has it or not. You know, usually, before the entertainer sings a note or speaks a word; just as you can tell, when a person picks up a violin, whether he is an accomplished performer or a rank amateur by the way he handles the instrument.

A person with stage presence is at ease, and makes his audience feel at ease as well. Nobody likes to see an awkward, inept, tentative person on a stage. It's embarrassing. Who has not had the experience of suffering through a song or dance or specialty where the performer forgot his lines, or muffed a cue, or dropped the plates he was juggling?

Nothing like that had happened with his girls, Bill thought, and nothing like that was likely to happen. They might make mistakes, but they had the happy faculty of putting the audience on their side immediately. All top entertainers and artists have that ability, and in the Lennon girls, the ability was natural. Each person in the audience felt as if they were singing to him and for him.

Such ability cannot be taught, Bill reflected, thinking back over his years in show business. Some of the greatest entertainers of all time were not the greatest singers, but they had in fullest measure the talent of winning an audience. Bill remembered a girl he had known, a girl with one of the finest soprano voices he had ever heard. She could have been a great star—but unfortunately she completely lacked stage presence. For some reason, audiences just didn't warm up to her. . . . I wonder what she's doing now? Bill thought.

The girls sang an encore. It was time for Bill and his brothers, who had planned to take part in the show's finale, to head backstage.

As he began to rise from his seat, he heard Sis whispering to him: "Bill! Where's Janet? She was in her seat a minute ago, but——"

There was an amused rustle in the audience. Dianne, Peggy, and Kathy, responding to generous applause, had launched into another number. But, suddenly, the trio had become a quartet. Janet, half asleep and knuckling her eyes, wandered onto the stage and joined in.

Bill chuckled. "I guess Janet couldn't bear to be left out of any excitement."

The older girls were obviously just as surprised as anyone else to see the addition, but it worked out beautifully. This small child had a voice which blended perfectly with the others.

The show's finale was sensational:

The girls' father and uncles and the girls themselves—all four of them—sang an old spiritual: "Dry Bones."

It brought down the house.

And that was the first public appearance of the four Lennon sisters.

They were offered other chances to sing before an audience, and one evening a month later, they received $20. After the show, they rushed up to their parents, their faces alight with glee. Dianne was triumphantly waving the check for $20—the first real money they had ever earned.

"Look! Look!" they shouted in chorus. "Twenty dollars! They *paid* us for singing!"

The girls found it hard to believe that someone would actually give them money, real money, for doing exactly the same thing they did every night over the dinner dishes. And such a vast sum too—twenty whole dollars!

"What are you going to do with it?" Sis asked.

"Do with it?" Dianne looked bewildered. "Why, give it to you, of course. The baby needs things, and——"

"But it's yours," Sis said gently. "You earned it."

"Well, you'd better take it, anyhow," Peggy said. "You know what to do with it better than we do, Mommy." The others nodded.

"All right, if that's the way you want it." Sis took the money and put it in her purse. "That's generous of you girls."

Spring turned to summer. The California hills turned from green to golden brown, and the famous California sun shone hot every day. School ended, and Dianne got a job with a local newspaper. It wasn't much of a job, and the pay check was small. But if it had been a check for a million dollars, Dianne's pride could have been no greater when she brought it home and handed it over to her mother.

Sis hid a smile at the sight of her eldest daughter acting like a weary breadwinner. "I'm tired after working all day," she said to Peggy and Kathy, who were plaguing her to play baseball. "You kids go play."

"You kids!" repeated Sis to herself, fondly, as Dianne curled up on the couch, for all the world like a business tycoon who has just put over a big deal. "You kids!"

High summer: July. Excursions to the beach, picnics, lazy evenings, simmering long days. Tuesday, July 20, 1954.

Sis Lennon was keeping pretty much to the house; another baby was due in a week, and a great deal of the household routine fell on the older girls. Little Mary, sixteen months old, was fretful at being cooped up, and Sis asked the other children to take the baby out in her stroller. All the children, with the exception of DeeDee, were out front. They took turns pushing the stroller containing little Mary up and down Garfield Avenue, on which the Lennon home faced. A quiet street, lined by small homes on narrow lots. Garfield Avenue doesn't go anywhere; there's no reason to drive along it unless you live there. If you live on Garfield Avenue, you know that usually, especially in summer, it's filled with children playing baseball or some other game. You know that, and you drive slowly and carefully.

For an hour Peggy, Kathy, Pat, and Danny wheeled the baby up and down, while little Mary fussed. She didn't like the heat.

"Let's let her out for a while," one of the children said, and lifted the baby from the stroller. Mary clung to her sister for a minute, then started to toddle along beside her.

Two other girls came skipping along, friends of the Lennon children. They exchanged "Hi's" and began to chatter.

They didn't see Mary, bored by standing still, cross the sidewalk and the curb and wander out into Garfield Avenue. She was there only a matter of seconds.

Sis Lennon came from the front door, looked at the girls, and saw that the baby was in the street. "Peggy! Kathy! Pat!" she called. "Get your little sister!"

There wasn't a car in sight. And then, suddenly, there was.

One turned the corner from Grandview Avenue, a street only one block long. It wasn't going especially fast, but Mary was only ninety feet from the corner. And the driver didn't see the tiny figure.

Sis screamed. Peggy and Kathy, panic-stricken, made desperate leaps. Kathy was closer, and the car missed her by inches.

It didn't miss the baby.

The next hours are a blur in the minds of Sis and Bill. Little Mary was rushed to the hospital, and Sis rode with her in the ambulance. It was too late, of course. A baby's fragile body meeting tons of steel can have only one result. Bill Lennon arrived at his home only minutes after the ambulance left. The police told him about the accident and he rushed over to the hospital. Little Mary was dead.

Over the happy home fell a veil. Someone who had been there was there no longer, and the house seemed empty and cold.

Only eight days later Bill, Junior, was born. Having a new baby in the house helped. But always, there was something to remind Sis and Bill of the other baby who had gone. Over and over they asked themselves: "Why did Mary die? Whose fault was it?"

Years later Bill Lennon said, "Those were the darkest months we ever knew—a tremendous emotional gap. Night after night I'd wake up to find Sis gone from bed. She would be rocking back and forth in the dark living room, crying to herself. I tried to comfort her, but it wasn't easy. Especially when I felt like crying myself."

There was no singing in the house that sad summer. The girls were quiet, grief-stricken, trying to help as best they knew how. Even the little boys would come up suddenly, throw their arms around their mother's neck, and give her an awkward kiss, to comfort her.

Gradually, gradually prayer and time, the great healers, brought their solace. The bereaved father and mother could say with quiet resignation, "Thy will, O Lord, not mine, be done."

Mary's image did not fade. It is still hard for them to talk of the little girl taken from them so suddenly and tragically, but the sharpest pain has receded. Even yet, Sis can often be seen looking at Mary's picture with misted eyes. She says:

"It was God's will. No one was to blame. I like to think there is a special little saint in Heaven, who is watching over us."

In time, life at the Lennons resumed its normal aspect. It was a long time, but life must go on. Dianne, Peggy, Kathy, little Janet began singing again as they worked around the house, or sat together on the front steps.

Sometimes one of the girls would say, "Let's sing one for little Mary," and their voices would rise in reverent harmony. They still sing for little Mary. And they are sure their little sister hears.

CHAPTER VII

Beyond the Mountains

Everyone has an enchanted place he remembers from childhood. It may be a farm or a summer home, a favorite vacation spot or simply a big back yard.

For the Lennon girls and their brothers, the enchanted place is Uncle Max's. In years to come, they probably will tell their children, a little wistfully, of the wonderful, magic days at Uncle Max's.

They are lucky. Max Heinrich, the brother of the graceful ballet dancer Bert Lennon met so long ago in Chicago, lives in one of the loveliest places in the United States—the California hill country. Most visitors to California never get to know the state's back country well, and this is a pity. For them, California means the endless fruit groves and vegetable farms near the coast; sprawling, brightly lighted Los Angeles; cool, charming San Francisco; maybe redwood trees, Yosemite, La Jolla, Hollywood, Disneyland—and miles of beaches, with the wide blue Pacific creaming in.

All this is beautiful. But there is another California, a country which has hardly changed since the brave mission fathers built their adobe chapels two centuries ago. This California is pleasingly quiet and remote. It is not a tourists' playground. People live quietly among their rounded hills, and never give a thought to Wilshire Boulevard or Vine Street.

And yet, it isn't far from the lights of Hollywood. Two or three hours' drive will take you into this other world. The air is clear and invigorating under a cloudless, bright blue sky. The hills are golden brown, with splashes of bright color where there are fields of blue lupine or California poppies. Here and there are patches and strips of dark green which are trees.

Far away rise the Sierras, true mountain country.

The grass and forests are full of little creatures who watch you with beady eyes. Birds are everywhere. Larger animals, too—fox, deer, coyotes, wildcats, even bears and an occasional panther.

There are brooks to wade in, trails to follow, woods to explore, hills to climb. A child can be an Indian or a cowboy, a pioneer or an explorer, all in one day.

The air doesn't have the mugginess of that near the coast, nor the sharp thinness of higher altitudes; it's perfect for doing things. The climate is neither too hot nor too cold. It rains only in winter, and there are no thunderstorms. There is no roar or screeching of traffic— the hills are quiet, except for the singing of birds.

Truly, a magic land for a child.

Of course, the Lennons always looked forward to a trip to Uncle Max's ranch. Max Heinrich and his wife, Aunt Helen, have an apricot and grape ranch near the town of Santa Paula, in Ventura County, about halfway between Los Angeles and Santa Barbara. Their fifty-five acres lie on both sides of Highway 150—rolling, hill country near the Topatopa range of mountains. The land is 1,550 feet above sea level at the entrance to the ranch, and slopes upward toward the mountains, which are very respectable mountains, indeed. They are part of the majestic Sierras, and not far from the ranch are peaks as high as 8,000 feet.

Max fits into these surroundings as if he had been born there. He wasn't—he has led a romantic, adventurous life and is now content to live out his years in the magic California hill country. Max was born in Munich, Germany, in 1898. When he was only a boy, he served in the German Army as a fighter pilot in World War I— one of those daring men who flew the flimsy box-kite planes of 40-odd years ago. Since then he has roamed the world over. Max is one of those men who can do almost anything. In his lifetime he has held many jobs in many countries. He is, among other things, a carver of ivory and a painter. It was as a free-lance artist that he came to California and worked for many of the large movie studios. Finally, he tired of the rush of city life, bought the ranch and settled down with Mrs. Heinrich. Naturally, Uncle Max has an endless wealth of stories—another reason why the Lennons are always overjoyed to visit the ranch in Ventura County.

On the first Saturday morning of summer vacation before the Lennons sang their first song for Lawrence Welk, Bill had an idea. He looked across the breakfast table at Sis, and then at the children on either side. "I have a couple of days coming," he said. "What do you say we take a little trip?"

"Swell!" the girls said in chorus, and Sis added: "It

would be nice. Where would you like to go?" Once more the chorus came:

"To Uncle Max's ranch!"

Bill laughed. "I thought that's what you'd say. You kids have all been working pretty hard in school, and Mother's working hard here at home, and I've been a little tired lately. I think it would do us all good."

As usual in such a situation, the girls began to chatter at once, until Bill had to rap his spoon on his coffee cup for attention. "Pipe down and listen!" When quiet was restored, he went on:

"Today you girls help Mother around the house. Tomorrow, after Mass, we'll start out in the car and get to Uncle Max's in time for lunch."

"How about the tires on the car?" Sis asked. "This tribe is a pretty heavy load."

Bill grinned. "I just checked them. They'll hold out."

Janet and the little boys piled up so much baggage for the three-day trip that Sis had to remind them they were going only about ninety miles, not taking a trip around the world. Each had a pile of favorite toys, dolls, or something which just *had* to go, but finally their mother reduced the load to manageable proportions.

Early Sunday morning they were up, dashing around excitedly. Early Mass, a hearty breakfast, some last-minute matters and they were on their way. A bright summer day. The girls sang as Bill drove north along the famous coast road, U.S. 101, one of the most scenic highways in the world. Past beach towns, winding between frowning cliffs and the blue ocean, with a few ships far away toward the horizon, like toys. Once they had to stop for a state trooper's signal—there had been a slide from the cliffs, and the road was partly blocked with boulders. A bulldozer was busily pushing the boulders off the road.

"Golly!" breathed Janet in awe. "S'posing one of those rocks had hit a car!"

Through the pretty town of Ventura, then inland to the village of Santa Paula. They were near Uncle Max's now, and the children were calling out to each other in excitement as they recognized familiar landmarks. At last, "There's Uncle Max's!" they all called. And there was the ranch, with Uncle Max and Aunt Helen standing near the door, smiling and waving.

The kids swarmed down from the car, greeted their great-uncle and great-aunt, and immediately scattered to their favorite places. Dianne and Janet made a beeline for their friend Pal, the white horse; the little boys ran for the tractors; Peggy and Kathy went to investigate the possibility of apricot or grape jam in the kitchen.

"So glad you came," Aunt Helen said, kissing Sis. "The children always love the ranch so."

"And so do we," Sis said. "It's such a change for us. Um-m-m! Just breathe that air!"

"They'll have big appetites, that's one sure thing," Uncle Max said. "How's lunch coming?"

"Ready in a minute," Aunt Helen said cheerfully, and went into the house. In a little while Uncle Max's shout brought the children running in for a big country lunch.

"Uncle Max," Janet asked, "sometime can I go hunting with you on the horse?"

Hunting was one of Uncle Max's great pleasures. He

liked to sling a bag of jerky and some hard bread behind the saddle, take a gun, and ride his horse into the empty Topatopa Mountains. He has often said that the panoramic view of the valley, after he reaches the snow-patched peak, is worth the strenuous climb. Everyone has his own frontier in his mind, and Uncle Max seems to have an inner thirst, a craving to see what lies beyond the mountains. To some it always seems that life's great adventures are on the other side.

Aunt Helen couldn't understand it—but then, few women can understand a man's yearning to get away by himself in the wilds. "Why," she said, "we have so many deer here they walk right onto the ranch, bold as brass, and nibble our apricot trees and grapes! And Max has to go away off into those mountains to hunt them!"

But now, in answer to Janet's question, Max shook his head. "Some day, honey. But right now it's dangerous." He lowered his voice. "Did you know there's a wild hypotenuse in those mountains?"

Dianne, Peggy, and Kathy giggled—although Janet wasn't quite sure she should—but the eyes of Janet and the little boys grew round. "What's a hitto—a hypo—what you said?" Danny asked.

"It's a strange beast, Danny, and the strangest thing about him is that he can't go anywhere in a straight line. So when you're hunting the wild hypotenuse, you have to figure out where he wants to go, and then go hunting for him someplace else."

"Oh," Danny said, not understanding.

"He comes from the country of Geometry," Dianne explained. "We studied about him in school."

98

Everyone laughed, and Bill explained about the hypotenuse. The meal ended with homemade jam on homemade bread—greatly to the satisfaction of Peggy and Kathy—and it was exploring time.

"Don't go too far," Sis said, confident that no harm could come to the children on Uncle Max's ranch.

"We'll watch the little ones," Dianne and Peggy both promised, and the older folks settled down to talk.

For the children, an enchanted afternoon. The golden light slanted down from the west, throwing sharp black shadows in the folds of the hills. High, high above, a hawk floated on motionless wings. Smaller birds sang and soared.

"I think," Janet said thoughtfully to Kathy, "that we are cave-people, and there's nobody else lives within thousands of miles, and Danny and Pat are my cave-children."

"That's a good idea," her sister said gravely. "But watch out for the dinosaurs."

"I will," Janet promised, running off happily with the little boys trailing her like a tail to a kite.

Dianne, Peggy, and Kathy stood looking at the mountains to the north—remote, unchanging, aloof. "Doesn't it make you feel kind of—kind of small, like a little ant or something?" Peggy asked.

Dianne nodded. "I always think those mountains were here long before people, and they'll be here, maybe, long after people. Do you suppose they see us, Kathy, and wonder what such little things are good for?"

For a while they pretended to be mountains, lofty and grand, who watched the antics of human beings and commented on them. Then this palled. They forgot they were serious young women, and ran off after Janet and the boys, who had stopped being cave men and were hunting for beavers by the little mountain brook on the north forty acres. They found frogs, but no beavers, and when the bigger girls came up, decided to dam up the little stream with rocks. Kathy dipped her toes into the water and shuddered. "Yikes, it's *cold!*"

Suddenly there was a scream of fright from Danny, a loud splash, and a wail of despair from Pat. The little boys had been playing follow-the-leader along the bank. Pat, paying more attention to the game than to where he was going, had tumbled into the icy water.

"Oh, golly!" shrieked Janet. "He'll drown!"

"Hush!" said Dianne. "The water's only two feet deep." Forgetting about the chill of the water, she plunged in to help her brother. Pat's face, more startled than anything else, appeared above the water and he opened his mouth to yell.

"Come on, young fellow," Dianne said, hauling him upright. "Everything's fine. DeeDee'll take care of you."

Dripping, unhappy, and scaring the frogs with his howls, Pat was set up on the bank. "We better get him back," said Kathy, practically. "He'll catch cold. So will you, DeeDee. Your clothes are all wet."

The little procession wound back toward Uncle Max's house, with Dianne carrying Pat, Janet skipping ahead like a drum major, and Danny, snuffling, bringing up the rear. Sis, hearing the commotion, came rushing out. "What's the matter?" she gasped.

"A little wetting," Dianne called cheerfully. "Nothing to worry about, Mother."

"Nobody ever catches cold in Ventura County," Uncle Max said.

And no one did. . . . Such little adventures were part of the magic of the ranch. Then, at night, after dinner, with the stars blazing in a velvet sky, was song time.

Aunt Helen's eyes were wet with tears as the girls sang together in the clear California night. Not popular songs, but old favorites, songs which never go out of date: "Annie Laurie," "Sweet Molly Malone," and their great-aunt's favorite, "Love's Old Sweet Song."

The young voices blended, and Aunt Helen whispered to Sis, "I'm as proud of them as if they were my own."

Sis smiled. "They are your own. They look on the ranch as their second home."

Then story time. And, as always, Peggy said:

"Tell us about Grandma, Uncle Max."

Uncle Max chuckled. "Grandma to you, Kitten, but my big sister Barbara to me. When I was very small, Barbara seemed almost as big as my father and mother. Then, you know, she went away with the dancing troupe, on the trip when she met your granddad, Bert.

"I didn't see her for years. When I did we were both grown, and I thought, My! How little Barbara has become! She could have walked under my arm. But she still told me where to head in!"

He told again the girls' favorite story: The first time Barbara Lennon had visited her brother's ranch, she was terrified by the silence, the remoteness, the lack of neighbors, the strange sounds at night. She was even terrified of the shotgun Max kept ready to shoot marauding hawks or coyotes.

Next day he and Aunt Helen drove to Santa Paula, leaving Barbara alone. It was fall, and Uncle Max had a sign on his front gate:

FRESH FRUIT FOR SALE AT THE HOUSE

"On our way back, we passed a car driving at a great speed, with a man in it looking scared to death. Later, we found out what had happened: The poor young fellow undoubtedly had driven in to buy some fruit. My sister Barbara thought he was a robber. She got the shotgun and jumped out at him. He was shocked to be looking into the business end of a shotgun, and he must have thought she was a madwoman. Without a word, he drove down the long lane like a streak of lightning."

"She was always like that," Bill Lennon said reflectively. "I don't think she ever weighed more than a hundred and five pounds soaking wet, but when we needed it she'd whack any of us, quickly—three or four times before you could duck once. We took it, too—meekly!"

"Did you ever get whacked, Daddy?" Janet asked.

He laughed. "When I needed it."

Every year on her birthday, Jack, her oldest son, would pick up his mother and put her on the table. She danced there, while her sons clapped in rhythm and shouted. "She never lost the grace she had when she was a young girl," Uncle Max said. "Even when she was past sixty, there was still much of the fire she had when she was eighteen."

It was getting late. Janet yawned and drooped. So did the others.

"End of the line for tonight," Sis said.

It was a gorgeous night, which had begun with a flaming sunset that painted the whole western sky in a riot of red and orange. Who would sleep under a roof on such a night? Not the Lennon girls! Uncle Max had built a neat bungalow a short distance from the main house just for the Lennons, but with the blue heavens so near, they decided to sleep in the open. Cots and blankets were ready alongside the house, and they said good night, recited their prayers, and snuggled under the blankets.

Quiet, except for the whirring and scraping of insects, a faraway chorus of frogs, and the occasional song of a night bird.

"DeeDee?"

"What is it, Peggy?"

"Are you asleep?"

"No. . . . Not quite. Why?"

"I was just thinking. Would you like to live at the ranch all the time?"

"Gee, I don't know. It's swell, but maybe it's best to save it for once in a while. That way we enjoy it more."

"I'd like to live here all the time," Kathy said. "Maybe I will. I'll be an artist."

"I'll live with you," said Janet sleepily, "and go hunting for hoppo—hypo—those things Uncle Max said." She sat up suddenly. "Hey, will bears come down and eat us?"

"If any bears come," Dianne assured her, "I'll let them eat me, and you can go get Uncle Max."

"O.K.," said Janet. " 'Night."

Short silence, then Peggy said, "Do you s'pose God is watching us from up there, beyond all those stars?"

"Sure. I don't know whether He's beyond the stars, but He's watching us. You know that." Kathy's voice.

"I wonder," pondered Peggy. "I want to do what He wants me to do, but I don't know yet. Do you think God wants me to be a nun?"

Dianne spoke, the big sister, the one to whom they always listened. "You'll know what God wants you to do when the time comes, Peggy. Meanwhile, all we can do is be good, and help Mother, and pray."

"I guess you're right, DeeDee."

Another short silence. Drowsily, from Janet: "Did the bears come yet?"

"No, honey. Hardly any."

"O.K. . . ."

And the clear, star-blazoned night swung above them as the tired girls slept.

In the morning they awakened just after dawn to the appetizing aroma of bacon, eggs, and coffee. Another day of adventure, another evening of singing and stories, another night of sleepy talk and rest.

Magic days, in an enchanted country. Lucky children, who have an Uncle Max and an Aunt Helen! Some day, long, long years away, other young ears will be listening to the stories about the ranch in Ventura County, the day Pat fell into the brook, and about Pal, the white horse.

The golden mountains will still be there, and the stars will still twinkle high above, in a purple velvet sky.

CHAPTER VIII

Housewarming

The long summer passed. There were other trips to Uncle Max's ranch, other family outings together—to the beach, to the desert country, to the mountains. Then came fall, and the eventful telephone call from young Larry Welk, Jr., which led to the invitation to appear on Lawrence Welk's Christmas TV show.

It soon became apparent that the quiet life of the Lennon family had changed. Welk invited them back again and again. Their popularity soared. The girls became regulars on the show. In a few short months they were what entertainment people call "good property"— they were being eagerly sought out for engagements and recording dates. It was well for them that Lawrence Welk had protected them with a contract! The girls' father was besieged by offers of agents and promoters, some legitimate, some only trying to make a fast buck by cashing in on the popularity of the Lennon girls. Sam Lutz, their personal manager, advises Mr. Lennon and the girls in all their business deals.

There were some things that required getting used to. For the four sisters it was strange and a little embarrassing, at first, to have people they had never seen before hail them by name in a store or on the street. Shortly after the Christmas show, Dianne and Peggy went on a shopping trip into Los Angeles. A girl rushed up to them in the store, said, "Why, Dianne and Peggy Lennon! How are you? Gee, it's good to see you!"

"We're fine," Dianne answered a little startled. "How are you?"

"Oh, swell," the girl said, and launched on a torrent of chatter that ended, somehow, with the three girls having sodas at the store's soda fountain. When the other girl finally shook their hands warmly and left, Peggy turned to Dianne and said, "She's nice, DeeDee, but why didn't you introduce me to your friend?"

"*My* friend!" cried Dianne. "Why, I never saw her before in my life! I thought she was *your* friend!"

Television stars all report the same thing: people greet them as if they had known them all their lives. There is something intimate about the little TV screen, which brings famous personalities into the nation's living rooms, that makes everyone look on his favorite stars as friends. Persons who wouldn't dream of rushing up and shaking hands with a stage star, for instance, will call a television actor by his first name.

Not that the Lennon girls mind. Not long ago Kathy said, "It's nice to feel we have so many friends!" And friends they are, although they might never meet, except through the medium of television.

Shortly after they had begun to appear regularly on his show, Lawrence Welk talked soberly to the girls about the problems that come with being well-known personalities.

"Never forget," he said, "how temporary a thing fame is. People see us every week, hear our music. Millions throughout the country know who the Lennon sisters are.

"But in a few short years, girls, you and I will be forgotten. There will be others taking our places. It might be twenty years, or ten, or even five. Sometimes that's hard to take. The most pathetic thing I know is a man or woman who was famous once, and isn't any more, but who still longs for the bright lights and recognition he once knew."

The girls nodded, and Dianne said, "We read a poem in school about a king in ancient times, who was very powerful and rich. But he was very humble too, and he had a servant whose only job was to whisper to the king every little while, 'Even this will pass away.' He wanted to be reminded that he was only mortal."

"Oh, that's sad!" Janet said, and Lawrence laughed.

"No, it isn't sad. In years to come, you will find other interests to fill your lives. Who knows? One of you may dedicate her life to God. Or you may have children, and you will know then that all the fame in the world isn't as satisfying as having a child come up and throw his arms around you."

But the girls found that it was nicer to spend more time at home than in public, where they were followed by whispers and nudges. With the money that came in from their appearances with Lawrence Welk, they were able to help their parents buy a larger house.

In December 1956 they moved from the little Garfield Avenue home where the family had lived for ten years and which was the only home the younger ones knew.

They waved good-by a little sadly, and there were tears in their eyes. But, after all, it wasn't as if they were moving to a strange city. The new house was only a few blocks from the old one. They were still in St. Mark's parish, only one short block away.

It wasn't a mansion. None of the Lennons would have been comfortable in a palace. The new home was much bigger than the old one, with seven bedrooms and two bathrooms. (This last feature delighted the girls. Peggy said: "At last! Now Kath can spend all day in the bathroom if she wants to and we won't have to hammer on the door!" Kathy is notorious for monopolizing the bathroom.)

There was plenty of room for everybody. To the Lennon girls, accustomed to the snug little house on Garfield Avenue, the blue-shuttered white house seemed huge. Janet said joyfully, "I got *lost* in it!" This was perhaps an overstatement, but there is no question about its roominess. Dianne and Peggy share a bedroom, so do Kathy and Janet. The four boys—Danny, Pat, Billy, and Joe—have two rooms; Bill and Sis have the master bedroom, and even little Mimi has a small room of her own. Mrs. Lennon's mother has a room which she uses on her frequent visits.

The house stands on a corner, on a sizable lot, which allows for a big back yard. The yard is surrounded by a high board fence, and makes an ideal baseball diamond, football field, Indian encampment, or anything.

Bob Wilson—a fireman by night—works for Bill Lennon during the day. He has done a great deal of work on the Lennon house since they moved in. Among other things, he has built bookcases, shelves, and cabinets, installed floodlights high overhead in the back yard, and constructed a patio and shrine. His creative ability has enhanced the appearance and convenience of this charming forty-year-old house.

Those refinements were still to come in the early part of 1957, shortly after the Lennons moved in, but the house was newly furnished and decorated. Inevitably, someone—later they weren't quite sure who—said, "Let's have a housewarming!"

The idea was so natural, and such a good one, that everybody agreed enthusiastically at once. Bill's brothers and their families were invited, and also the neighbors. Guests of honor were Lawrence and Fern Welk, their son Larry and daughter Donna, and a friend they have known for years, the Reverend Joel Gromowski.

Everybody brought small gifts for the new house—just trifles, but enough to make the little children feel as if Christmas had come all over again. They all gathered together in the back yard, following the southern California tradition which says that no one must stay indoors when he can be outside.

"Plenty of room for a ball game in this yard," Welk said, nodding approvingly. "Especially if we use a plastic whiffle ball."

A whiffle ball is a ball about four inches in diameter, hollow and pierced with holes. The ball cannot be thrown fast and doesn't go far when it is batted, but the holes make it perform all sorts of odd antics in the air. A game played with the plastic ball is full of surprises.

Bill Lennon laughed. "We have a whiffle ball, and it's

a good day for a game," he said. "I suppose you're itching for revenge, Lawrence. Your team was clobbered the last time, as I remember."

"Seven to one!" Lawrence replied dolefully. "But I have a feeling today will be different. Can we have the same teams?"

"I think so. You were captain and pitcher for the Venice Wildcats."

"That's right, and we had Father Joel, Peggy, Kathy, Danny, your brothers Ted and Jim—let's see—oh, yes, and your brother Pat."

"My Champion Sluggers had Dianne, Janet, your son Larry, my brother Tom, Jim's son and daughter, and Len Kelley. You're in for a tough game!"

In a little while the game was organized, and the "bleachers"—camp chairs on the patio—were full of a rooting section including the women and small children. Sis turned thumbs down on the suggestion of a full nine innings because there was too much food to be eaten, so Lawrence and Bill agreed on a five-inning game. Then Monsignor Wade, pastor of St. Mark's, came in and was drafted into service as umpire.

"I don't know whether I should," he said. "Nobody likes the ump. If they start throwing pop bottles, I quit!"

They assured him that partisan violence would be held to a minimum, and with the Sluggers at bat, having won the toss, the game started. Janet, lead-off man, weighed only seventy pounds, but she was a tiger at the bat. On the second pitch the ball whizzed past Welk's head, and she stood on first, flushed and laughing.

Jim's daughter popped out, but Dianne, after waiting

out a full count, whacked a hard hit ground ball through Welk's legs for a double, sending Janet to third.

"Take him out!" jeered the bench. "Back to the showers for the pitcher!" Little Danny came in from second base, and he and Lawrence conferred solemnly, exactly like big leaguers in the World Series. "Just calm down," Danny advised him. "Take it easy, Mr. Welk. Don't let 'em razz you. Just wait till we get up to bat!"

Welk nodded, trying to look worried. "They've got plenty of power up there," he said. "This is a dangerous game, Danny."

Larry flied out when a puff of wind sent the ball into the hands of Pat Lennon, but Bill Lennon got a hit which scored Janet and Dianne. Then Jim's son rolled to first, and the Sluggers were out.

Danny, up first for the Wildcats, waved his bat fiercely, and got a solid hit. Then came Peggy.

"Here's an easy out!" shouted Janet, capering in the infield.

"Pitch to her, Daddy!" called Dianne. "Pitch to her! Peg couldn't hit the water if she fell out of a boat!"

Mrs. Lennon said, "That's not nice," but Peggy only grinned and said, "They don't bother me. I admit I'm the Hitless Wonder. Where the ball is, my bat isn't."

She took a wicked cut at the ball and knocked it into a gutter on the roof, and the game had to be called while Bill scrambled up a ladder to retrieve it. But she kept her title as the "Hitless Wonder" by knocking a little pop fly to her father.

So the game went, through four hard-fought innings.

Nobody was quite sure what the ball would do next. Sometimes it performed a little jig in the air as the breeze caught it. A pitch would slow down unaccountably, or develop an erratic curve, or a throw in from the outfield would swerve like a boomerang. Such things happen with a plastic ball. It was a wild, frantic, ridiculous game—but it was a lot of fun.

All players had at least one hit, with the exception of Peggy. The outstanding catches had been made by Father Joel, up against the wall in center field.

The atmosphere grew tense as inning succeeded inning. First the Sluggers scored, then the Wildcats. Finally, the Wildcats came to bat in the last of the fifth inning, with the score tied, 4–4. Their last chance!

"A tie game would be almost as bad as losing," Danny said. "Come on, gang! We gotta get a run!"

Monsignor Wade, who had made some close decisions, started quoting "Casey at the Bat": "The outlook wasn't rosy for the Mudville nine that day. . . ."

Danny Lennon stepped to the plate and belted the first pitch for a clean hit. He stole second as Pat flied out to the left fielder, then made a third on a sacrifice by Welk. Two down—and Peggy, the Hitless Wonder, coming to bat!

Somebody talked about a pinch hitter, but Welk shook his head. "No. Everybody takes his turn. Peggy can do it."

"C'mon, Sis!" implored Danny from third base.

Grimly she tapped the plate. Ball one. Foul—strike one. Strike two, a clean miss. Then Bill Lennon went into an elaborate windup and the ball came floating over the plate. Whack! The ball sailed into the air, seemed to hang up there irresolutely. Danny streaked for home. Dianne waited under the ball, her arms outstretched. "Got it!" she shrieked—too soon. A breath of air caught the ball, it wobbled, touched her hands, and fell. The Wildcats had been revenged—and Peggy, the Hitless Wonder, was the heroine of the day!

"Never mind!" Janet said consolingly to Dianne. "We'll have our turn. Wait till the next game!"

But the game was over, and it was time for the players to restore their strength with the dinner Sis had cooked. Watching them as they tore into the buffet table, Sis laughed and shook her head. "See why our food bills are so high?" she said to Fern Welk.

"I certainly do! My goodness, how much milk do you use, Sis?"

"We average ninety-one quarts a week. Just watch it disappear!"

Hamburgers, thin-sliced ham, rolls, salad, potato chips and potato salad, milk, vanished as the hungry crew ate.

Then it was time for singing. First it was the turn of the Lennon brothers—Bill, Jim, Pat, and Ted—who took their hearers back to the days of the late thirties and early forties.

"Haven't forgotten a line of the old ones!" Bill said. "Once you learn a song, it's yours for life."

Their audience applauded. Mrs. Welk said, "Now it's the turn of the younger generation. How about it, girls?"

"Golly," Dianne said with a shake of her head, "I hate to follow them. We'll sound pretty bad by comparison."

"Indeed, you won't," Lawrence Welk told her. "They're good, all right, but you're good too!"

So the girls stood up and sang several numbers. Then it was everyone's turn. Even the smaller children joined in, singing old songs which everyone knew and loved, while the scarlet sun sank lower and twilight came.

Finally, the guests left, thanking the Lennons for a wonderful time. The little ones were put to bed, and the girls, yawning, followed them shortly. Bill and Sis, cleaning up after the party, exchanged smiles. They didn't have to speak; each knew what the other meant: "It was fun. It's wonderful to have such a nice family and friends. We have much to be thankful for."

Did the Sluggers get their revenge? Certainly! There have been many more such parties and ball games in that big back yard. Many more informal singing parties. The home is a center of love, life, and laughter—and, after all, that is what a home is for.

CHAPTER IX

Golden Days

At the foot of the folded mountains which rise above the town of Sierra Madre, California, sits a cluster of Spanish-style buildings. The buildings belong to the Passionist Fathers and constitute their famed Retreat House. It is an ideal place for people to go and shed, for a few hours, the noise and cares of the world. The stillness, unbroken except for the songs of birds; the solemn grandeur of the golden hills and purple-shaded valleys; and the gardens of the religious community all combine to turn one's thoughts toward eternal things.

For many years, Bill and other members of the family have made periodic retreats to Sierra Madre. Among the fathers who conduct the Retreat House is their intimate friend, the Reverend Joel Gromowski, C.P., assistant rector.

I knew that Father Joel had watched the Lennon girls grow up. He had known them long before there was any idea they would gain nationwide fame. I wanted to find out from him what he thought about the girls, and how they had weathered the inevitable changes which come with being so well known.

Father Joel shook my hand heartily and led me to a

quiet place in a walled garden. "My favorite spot," he said. "There's nothing to be seen from here which reminds me of today's world. Sometimes I like to imagine I'm one of the early friars who came to California centuries ago, like Fray Junipero Serra." He broke off and laughed as a flight of jets droned high overhead. "You can't stay in the eighteenth century very long!

"The Lennons," he said thoughtfully. "Well, I'll tell you about those girls. They're like nieces to me. I've known them for years—they're a fine family. You know, sometimes the noise and chatter of a bunch of children is a good antidote for the contemplative life, and I always get plenty of noise and chatter when I visit Bill and Sis."

Father Joel had been away in Mexico City for almost two years, he said, sent there by his superiors on a special mission.

"When I left, the girls were just average kids. They used to sing, of course, and I was always delighted to hear them. But it never entered my mind that they would go into the entertainment business. I don't know why I didn't think of it. I don't see many shows, or watch television, but I knew they were talented.

"Anyhow, when they tried out with Lawrence Welk, they wrote me all about it. They were thrilled, of course, and I wrote back wishing them good luck. Then it developed they were going to be a fixture on the show and apparently were launched on a career as singers."

Father Joel frowned a little, plucked a flower and twirled it absently between his fingers. "I wasn't entirely happy. I had the greatest trust in the girls and their parents, but I knew what could happen. After all, they were only youngsters—still are. And Hollywood holds a terrific temptation for much older heads than theirs.

"Up here, in the Retreat House, we hear many stories. We're so close to Los Angeles and Hollywood that a great many people connected with the movies and television come to us."

He paused a moment, then went on. "I don't deny I was worried about them while in Mexico. It seemed to me they had been catapulted from obscurity into fame without having had a chance to acclimate themselves. I hoped they wouldn't gradually get a more worldly, material outlook on life. I hoped the money they were earning and the popularity they had won wouldn't change them into something different from what they were."

He smiled. "I needn't have worried. When I returned, I called Bill and made a date to go out to their home— they'd just moved into the new one, and he said they were all anxious for me to see it. When I was driving along on the way to Venice, I had visions of Dianne in a flashy kind of dress like the screen stars frequently wear, and Peggy in one of those ridiculous outfits you some-times see along Hollywood Boulevard—silly ideas. Well, when I arrived there, they came roaring out of the house like bees out of a hive, the whole tribe of them, all trying to get to me first. I knew then I needn't have worried at all."

Had he noticed anything at all different about them?

"Well—no, not really. The girls were two years older and more poised and mature, but that was natural and would have happened if they'd never sung a note.

"But I could tell right away that none of them had

lost that glow of freshness and innocence that they'd had when I left, and I thanked God for it. Oh, I don't mean they were full of false modesty, or anything like that— any such pretense would have saddened me. They all talked at once, about what fun they were having and where they were going to sing, and how swell Lawrence Welk is, and so on. I could hardly sort out all the chatter.

"They were bursting to tell me everything that had happened, but the point is, you see, they were happy and proud and wanted me to share their happiness. Which I did. I didn't notice a trace of any false sophistication or conceit or that abnormal self-centeredness which overcomes many whose names go up in lights.

"Five minutes after I arrived Janet was wrestling with two of her brothers on the lawn, and Kathy had found a caterpillar and was trying to drop it down Peggy's back. When I saw that, I lost my fear that they had 'gone Hollywood.' "

Father Joel, a pleasant-faced man in his thirties, frequently visits the Lennons.

"Sometimes," he said, "a priest feels himself in an awkward place when he visits a house. Some people are never entirely at ease with a priest. They become stilted and stiff in their actions, and that makes the poor priest feel stilted and stiff and throws a pall over the whole visit. Whenever that happens, I feel it best for all to excuse myself.

"Others—not many, but some—go to the other extreme. In their anxiety to make the visiting priest feel that he is a member of the family, they forget the respect due

his office. When this happens, too, I excuse myself cour-
teously as soon as I can."

Father Joel said the Lennons made neither of those
mistakes. They were friendly and cordial, and the children
especially made him feel as if he were their favorite uncle,
but they never overstepped the bounds of propriety.

He recalled a visit he had paid to them on a holiday in
spring. They had planned a golf outing for some time—
Father Joel is an enthusiastic golfer, although not exactly
in Ben Hogan's class. Bill, Dianne, and he were to make
up a threesome at Rancho Golf Course, not far from their
Venice home.

Dianne, a splendid natural athlete, is the best golfer
of the girls. While of course she cannot compare with
men in strength, she has enough skill and dexterity to be
able to compete on fairly even terms on the golf course.

"I found that out!" Father Joel laughed. "I whaled
away at my first drive and got about two hundred yards.
The only drawback was that it sliced onto Number Three
Fairway. Bill landed in a trap, but Dianne poled hers
a hundred and eighty yards straight down the middle. I
overshot my second, and don't know where Bill landed,
but Dianne took a Number Two wood and laid the ball
right on the apron of the green."

At the end of the out nine, Bill was ahead four strokes
but had lost the last two holes to Dianne. He said,
"DeeDee, you can't beat me another hole today."

"I think I can, Dad. I feel lucky."

"If you do, I'll give you three new golf balls!"

Father Joel said he was three down as they teed up for
Number Ten. "I told Dianne, 'Being a good golfer is the

sign of a misspent youth.' Bill said his father had always advised him never to play cards with a man named Doc and never to shoot pool with a man in a green eyeshade. Dianne only giggled, and kept right on hitting them straight down the fairway."

Father Joel remembered that as they waited their turn on a tee, an elderly man asked her if she was Dianne Lennon.

"She said yes, and the man told her how much he and his wife enjoyed her and her sisters' singing. She autographed his scorecard and introduced her father and me, and thanked him. Very nice and courteous, she was—neither condescending, the way some stars get, nor pulling that 'How did you ever recognize poor little me?' stuff. I was proud of her."

Bill had kidded him about being beaten by a girl, but Father Joel managed to pull even in the back nine and they went into the eighteenth with Father Joel and Dianne even. Bill was out in front eight strokes. Father Joel, like all golfers, never forgets a hole. The eighteenth is 395 yards, par four.

"I was in trouble right away and never did get out. Dianne drove behind a clump of bushes and had to chip back onto the fairway, losing some yardage. Bill thought he had it sewed up on the last hole when he used a five-iron to get on in two. Dianne made a wonderful recovery with a three-iron and was on in three, but she lay about twenty-five feet from the pin, with an uphill putt.

"Well, anyhow, Bill took three putts to sink his ball. Dianne studied for a minute and then made one of the most beautiful putts I've ever seen—dead in for a par

The girls welcome a new member of the family.

The Lennon family and the new addition. Left to right, front row: Kathy, Pat, Mimi, Billy, baby Anne in her mother's arms, and Peggy. Left to right, back row: Janet, Dianne holding Joey, Mr. Lennon, and Danny.

The girls help out in the kitchen.

The Lennon sisters practice, with Kathy at the piano.

Dianne's and Peggy's bedroom

Kathy's and Janet's bedroom

Kathy swings at a fast one as Dianne, Janet, and Peggy watch.

Peggy and Kathy enjoy their favorite sport, swimming.

The Lennon girls get together with Lawrence Welk.

net gets help from her sters and Lawrence Velk as she studies her atechism.

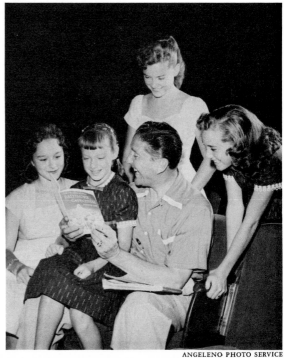

Dianne, Janet, Kathy, and Peggy enjoy a laugh with Lawrence Welk during a break in rehearsals.

The Lennon sisters with the Lawrence Welk Glee Club

Dianne, Kathy, Peggy, and Janet with Lawrence Welk at a concert
at Buckley Ranch in Indiana

The Sweethearts of Song

DIANNE

KATHY   PEGGY

JANET

four. So both of us big strong men were beaten on the last hole by a mere girl. Although, as Dianne said, girls aren't very 'mere' any more."

"You did beat me the last hole, DeeDee," said her father. "Here are the three new balls. Even shooting an eighty-three, I only beat you seven strokes."

For his next visit, Father Joel said, he made an imposing-looking "trophy" out of an old coffee can, and they had a little ceremony of presenting it to the golf champs.

"Dianne has a good sense of humor," Father Joel continued. "I told her not to let her pride get the better of her, and she said she owed all her golfing success to three rules: getting plenty of sleep, breathing deeply, and not following advice by amateurs." He laughed.

Another day and another visit, and the priest went with the Lennon family for a dip in the ocean. The entire Lennon family are at home in a swimming pool or an inland lake or tackling the rolling breakers of the world's largest ocean. They love to jump with the waves. By working your arms furiously when the waves reach their crest, or when the wave feathers at the top, you can body-surf a long distance.

This is great sport and the children are well trained. They are cautious; Bill has taught them to have no fear of the water, but to observe safety rules at all times.

They like water fights, choosing sides and splashing away until they are weak from laughter. "Kathy and little Janet took on Peggy and Dianne," Father Joel said. "It looked one-sided to me, so I gave my war cry and jumped in on the weaker side. I thought! They all ganged up on me. I felt as if I were standing under Niagara Falls."

They also have sand fights, with the entire family joining in a free-for-all battle until they collapse from laughter.

After all that exercise, it's pleasant to rest. Late afternoon on the glistening sand, watching the lazy rollers break and spread their foaming rugs on the beach, in and out, endlessly. Watching the sun turn red-orange, finally disappearing behind the wreath of cloud which always seems to hang just above a Pacific horizon. Lazy, friendly, cozy talk, with just enough freshness in the still warm air to be pleasant, while the sky turns from blue to purple and finally to that measureless dark blue in which the stars seem to be suspended.

"After that, it's always singing time," Father Joel explained. "That's the time I look forward to, more than any other. My voice—well, anyhow I can remember the words. But I don't mind joining in when they all are singing."

Anything the girls sing sounds good to Father Joel, although he confesses he prefers the "old-timers."

Each girl has a favorite and generally they go through the list: Dianne's "Funny Valentine," Peggy's "Sleepy Time Down South" and "Say It Isn't So," Kathy's "You'll Never Know" and "Did I Remember?" and Janet's pet, the hauntingly beautiful "You'll Never Walk Alone."

Then, while other people on the beach gather quietly and listen, they may turn to old songs. Lullabies which had been sung to each girl in turn and to their brothers and sisters after them: "Molly Malone" or Brahm's

"Lullaby." Maybe American folk tunes: "Beautiful Dreamer" or "Love's Old Sweet Song."

The spectators, who may or may not know who is singing, sometimes join in. Occasionally, one comes up, shyly, and asks if they are the girls who sing with Lawrence Welk.

Then, long after dark, with the little ones asleep, the family piles into the station wagon for the trip home.

"Those are wonderful days," Father Joel said in a dreamy tone. "Wonderful days." He seemed to come back to the present. "My, it's getting late." Shadows were creeping along the walls of the Retreat House. It was time he was about his duties. We rose to our feet and started out of the garden.

"If I live to be an old, old man," he said, "I'll always count those hours as among the most pleasant of my life. Sis and Bill have done a good job in raising their children. As I told you, they're just the same nice children I left when I went to Mexico. Sis told me once, 'We don't want them to go around with long faces all the time. There's no reason they shouldn't have fun, but we've tried to help them find their fun in wholesome ways.'

"Well," Father Joel said, "I think they've succeeded." He gave me a pleasant smile and walked away, humming Janet's favorite song:

> *"Walk on, walk on with hope in your heart*
> *And you'll never walk alone. . . ."*

CHAPTER X

Once in a Lifetime

There is something very special, very special indeed, about a high school Senior Prom. It is something like a farewell to childhood and not unlike a debut into society, or it could even be compared to a magic night from an ancient tale.

For most American youngsters it is a time that will be remembered always. Many a gray-haired grandmother will blink back a tear as she thinks of herself as she was, long ago, on that enchanted night. Even a gruff, balding elderly man will feel a glow as he thinks back over the years to the time when he was young, and so was the world, at the Senior Prom.

There have been dances before, and there will be many dances afterward. But not like that one. The Senior Prom is always *the* dance.

The first Prom for the Lennons came in May 1957. Dianne's, of course. But really, her family's too, for a wonderful event like that is something to share. Peggy, Kathy, and Janet were nearly as excited as Dianne. Even the little boys caught something of the feeling and Dan (The Man) was heard boasting to his awestruck playmates:

"My sister's goin' to the Prom!"

They weren't quite sure what the Prom was. Neither was Dan, but he knew it was something earth-shaking. And so it was. The first tremblings of the Prom had been heard shortly after New Year's, when senior committees were formed and school talk turned more and more to such things as orchestras, decorations, corsages, dates and —most important for the girls—"What will my dress be like?"

For Dianne, the choosing of a color was easy. It had to be blue, her favorite, a color which went stunningly with her blond beauty. But there are so many blues and so many kinds of dresses! Endless, delicious conversations with Sis and the other girls, while Bill tried to close his ears as he grumbled, "Woman-talk!"

But he was proud, nonetheless. Fathers are.

Dianne was going with Tom Capp, a long-time friend. She was (and still is, for that matter) fond of Tom, and he of her; but it was a cousinly fondness, with no overtones of puppy love. They liked each other's company, looked and danced well together, and knew they were going to have the time of their lives.

As The Day came closer, the excitement grew around the Lennon house until it was almost tangible. In self-defense Bill retreated to the practice-house in the back yard, where he could read or work on musical scores in peace. There was nothing but Prom in the house.

A week before the Prom, the phone rang. It was Tom, faced with the age-old problem of young escorts.

"Hi, DeeDee. I just called to find out what color dress you are going to wear. You know—for the corsage."

Oh, yes, she knew! "It's blue," she told him. "Between turquoise and iceberg."

"Oh." There was a small silence. "I thought an iceberg was white."

She gave a gurgle of laughter. "Don't be silly! It's—well," she went on dreamily, "sort of like the blue in the sky, 'way out over the ocean, early in the morning."

"Oh, fine!" Tom, like many another young swain, found himself far beyond his depth in discussing dress colors with a girl. "I'll just tell 'em to give me some flowers that look good on the sky. Or maybe it'd be better if I came over and took a squint for myself!"

"Don't you dare, Tom! I want it to be a surprise."

He laughed. "All right, but I'll say this—it's great to be a man and not have to worry about what color an iceberg is. Remember Hamlet? He wore 'customary suits of solemn black.' That's me!"

"Well, don't—— I mean, Tom, don't feel that you have to spend a—— After all, it isn't so important that——"

It's hard for a girl to tell a boy that he doesn't have to buy orchids, that she'll be happy with whatever he sends —as long as it goes with blue! But boys are notoriously color-blind and can't see what difference it makes if they send over a corsage of glaring orange flowers when a girl plans to wear pink.

"Calm down, DeeDee. You can trust your Uncle Tom, you know."

"I know," she said gratefully. "And thanks."

The other girls had been shamelessly eavesdropping. All's fair, in a Prom. "Gee," Janny said. "I betcha he sends a dozen orchids."

"Don't be silly!" Peggy said in a superior tone. "A dozen orchids!"

"It'd be awfully expensive too," said Kathy, practically. "I think he's going to send her gardenias."

DeeDee came in. "That was Tom," she announced, unnecessarily. "He was asking about my dress."

"DeeDee," pleaded little Janny, "try it on, huh?"

"Well . . ."

The others added their voices, and Sis Lennon said, "It might be a good idea, Dianne. After all, the dance is only a week away."

Dianne didn't need much persuasion. She ran upstairs and in a few minutes floated back, transformed from a kid in bermudas to a lovely young lady in a blue gown.

"Gee!" sighed Janny rapturously. "I'm gonna wear blue for *my* prom!"

Even Danny, who was inclined to make faces and groan when his sisters began to talk about clothes, was moved to produce a low whistle.

"It looks just beautiful, DeeDee," said Sis, a catch in her throat. "Beautiful!"

Dianne swayed and turned, to the applause of the family, then vanished to put the dress away until the big night. As she disappeared, Peggy said:

"Hey, you know I just thought of something! We won't have to practice the night of the Prom. I can catch up on some of those new records we haven't had a chance to play yet—Mantovani and Perry Como——"

Kathy said she was going to finish Jim Bishop's *The Day Christ Died*. Janet held out for a baseball game. But the idea of an evening with nothing to do was alluring.

Then, all of a sudden, it was Saturday—Prom Day. Sis turned thumbs down on plans of the small fry to sit on the steps and welcome Tom with an organized cheer.

"Out!" she said sternly. "Out of sight—yes, you too, Peggy and Kathy. This is Dianne's night. Your turn will come."

She relented enough to allow the girls to peek through the doorway when Tom came up the front walk, in the splendor of his dinner jacket, carrying a corsage box.

Bill greeted him. Tom, who knew the family of old, was lucky; he didn't face the fearful embarrassment that usually comes when a boy meets a girl's family on the night of a dance.

"Hi, Mr. Lennon," he said cheerily. "Hi, Mrs. Lennon. The Glamour Girl somewhere near ready?"

"A girl ready on time?" Bill grinned. "Tom, my boy, you have a lot to learn!"

"Dianne said you were doubling with Chuck Hunner and Marcie Glanville. Are they in the car, Tom?" asked Sis. They were. "Why don't you ask them to come in?"

"Well, they said they'd wait in the car. Confidentially, Mrs. Lennon, it took twenty minutes to get Marcie in, with that big flouncy dress, and the thought of doing it again——"

He broke off. Dianne was coming down the stairs, and Tom gave vent to an admiring whistle. "Hey, now!" he said. "You know, DeeDee, I thought you'd be wearing some old flour sack. You surprise me!"

This, in teen-age talk, is a real tribute.

Dianne, conscious of her new grown-up dignity, didn't

pay him back with a wisecrack, but only smiled sweetly and gave him her wrap.

"Oh—the flowers," Tom said, suddenly a trifle awkward. He handed her the box. Kathy had guessed right: gardenias, always in taste, blending perfectly with the light blue dress.

"Oh, they're lovely! Thank you, Tom," said Dianne, as her mother helped pin the corsage on the dress.

"Ah—Tom," said Bill. Like Tom, he felt just a little awkward. After all, it was his first prom, too—for a daughter. "I suppose you'll be going somewhere after the dance."

"We thought we'd go to the Albatross for a bite," Tom said. He grinned. "I think I know what you're going to say, Mr. Lennon. Well, don't worry. I'll drive carefully. I always do, and besides my folks would skin me alive if they knew I'd been speeding. And it wouldn't do to spoil those flowers, would it?"

Bill shook his hand. "I'll trust you, Tom. Have fun."

There was a flurry of good-bys. The other girls, unable to stay hidden, rushed out as Dianne and Tom left, and added to the uproar.

A magic night!

Clear, warm, spangled with stars, as such a night should be. High above, in the crystalline sky, the contrails of a Navy jet squadron drew white lines across the dark blue. Dianne thought the lines looked like musical staffs and the stars were notes. Far away, in Los Angeles, a battery of searchlights etched their silvery beams.

"Oh, golly," Dianne breathed, "what a night!"

What a night, indeed! A night to treasure in memory,

to be taken out and dreamed over years in the future. A once-in-a-lifetime night which, like all things that happen but once, is bittersweet with the thought:

"This once—this once, then never again!"

But at seventeen, on Prom Night, there is small room for reflection. The evening dissolved into a kaleidoscope of color, music, and dancing. The St. Monica High School Auditorium decorated—surely, decorated as no high school auditorium has been before, and the most absolutely wonderful orchestra in the world, playing music which was certainly inspired. The gay colors of the girls' dresses, the excited greetings, the admiring glances of the boys, and—sweetest of all—the glances of the other girls.

And Tom, suddenly almost a stranger in his black tie, circling the floor with Dianne in his arms. Then he grinned down, a companionable grin, and he wasn't a stranger any more, but only Tom as he said:

"I don't want to swell your head, or I'd tell you that you aren't absolutely repulsive. I've even seen a couple of girls more awful looking than you are."

Dianne giggled. She knew what this meant. A battery of poets with harps and lyres could bring forth no more heady praise.

"Never mind the talk," she said. "Just watch your two left feet."

Of such lighthearted insult is the modern-day boy-and-girl talk built. But they understand each other. The dance went on; slow numbers, fast ones, Latin music, even waltzes. The magic didn't fade.

Then, suddenly, the orchestra was playing the traditional "Good Night, Sweetheart." Someday a wise man will figure out how many times "Good Night, Sweetheart" has been played to wind up school dances, and how many hands are clasped a little tighter with the knowledge that a magic evening is closing.

"Sing it, DeeDee," Tom urged softly. "Go on."

"No," she whispered. "Not unless you sing it too."

Their voices joined, softly, and nearby couples danced close to listen. "Good night, sweetheart, 'til we meet tomorrow, good night, sweetheart, sleep will banish sorrow . . ."

And it was over. A sudden scurrying for wraps, a breathless round of "see you later," and they were out in the clear air again. But it was still Prom Night, and the night was still young.

There was so much to talk over, so much to say! At one of the young peoples' favorite spots, DeeDee and Marcie Glanville rushed off to freshen up while the boys secured a table and ordered chicken for all.

"Gee," Marcie said dreamily, "it was fun!"

"Uh-huh," Dianne said, just as dreamily, and they fell into a reverie.

From around them came the babble of other girls: "Did you see Bonnie and Jeannie, they had dresses just alike. . . . Didn't you just love Marsha's corsage. . . . Jim's a simply awful dancer, but he's lots of fun. . . ."

"I wish you were going to St. Mary's with me next fall, DeeDee." There was a note of sadness in Marcie's voice, a hint of knowledge that an era in their lives had ended.

"I do, too, in a way. But gosh, I'll be home with the family, and Mom needs me."

"I suppose you'll be busy with television. Gee, that

must be fabulous!" Marcie sighed. "With Lawrence Welk, and all!"

"Fabulous?" Dianne paused. "Oh, it's fun. And it's nice to be making money. But you know, Marcie, it doesn't seem awfully important. I mean——" Such thoughts are not easily expressed. "I mean, I'm not always going to be singing on television. I've got to think beyond that."

"Well, what?" Marcie demanded. "Tom Capp?"

Dianne shook her head. "No. I don't think so. . . . Tom's very nice, but he's really just a friend." She paused, looking at herself in a mirror, and wrinkled her forehead. "I just don't know. . . . I want to get married and have children of my own, and a home. That's what a girl's *for*, after all, isn't it? And I love babies so."

Marcie looked solemn. "Uh-huh. Gee, DeeDee, life's funny, isn't it? And complicated!"

"It sure is," Dianne said. She jumped to her feet. "Come on. The boys are waiting and I'm simply *starved!*"

. . . And so, finally, the magic night ended. But, in a sense, such nights never end. They still live and stay fresh, even after the years have brought other senior proms and other young girls in blue, waiting for a boy in a rented dinner jacket, carrying a corsage of gardenias.

Have we spent too much time with a high school prom? After all, there are thousands of them every year throughout this wide land, and there were thousands last year and there will be thousands next year.

What is so special about St. Monica High School, class of 1957?

Nothing, really.

Except that in an age when too much is written about the sad state of our young people, it's good to spend a little time with them in their happy days. Dianne Lennon happens to be one of the best known teen-age girls in the country. But aside from that, she was then a perfectly normal, ordinary high school girl.

This May, and next May, you could find hundreds of thousands of Dianne Lennons, from Bangor, Maine, to San Diego, California, living in a whirl of happiness, waiting for the prom.

It's good to live with them, on their magic night, the night that comes once in a lifetime.

CHAPTER XI

The Magic Carpet

So Dianne, with her senior prom behind her, emerged into adulthood. In that summer of 1957, the full impact of their changed status—full-fledged television stars—had not yet hit the four girls.

They began to have an inkling of what it means to be known the country over on some comparatively short personal appearance tours they made that summer with their father. They covered the West Coast—San Francisco; Portland, Oregon; and Spokane, Washington. In every town they were astonished to see the thousands of people who had seen them on TV, who greeted them like old friends, and who—in Portland—stood for hours in a pouring rain to wave and talk to them.

That Portland trip was the second one. On their first visit—with only an hour and a half layover between planes—there was a heart-warming incident.

The girls had friends there, friends they had never seen: the three girls of the Daniel Cason family. One of them, Shirleen, had written such a glowing fan letter to the Lennon girls after their first appearance on TV that Dianne answered. A correspondence was started between the quartet in Venice and the three girls in Portland. Each set of sisters was eager to meet the other.

The Lennons' plane landed in Portland at the unearthly hour of 5 A.M.—and there were all the Casons, wide-awake and eager, waiting to meet them. It was a meeting of old friends, and the young people chatted happily away.

One of the Lennon girls—afterward they couldn't remember which one, but it didn't matter because they were all thinking the same thing—invited the whole Cason family to Venice. "Spend Christmas with us!" the girls pleaded. The invitation was so obviously sincere that the Cason girls happily accepted. (There is a footnote to the story: The Casons did come to California, and stayed for two weeks. Later, as a result of seeing how the Lennon family lived, the Casons embraced Catholicism. "We just had to," Shirleen said, "after we saw how they lived. It was such a happy and satisfying life!")

On another trip they spent several days in San Francisco, a city as different from Los Angeles as if it were on the other side of the country instead of in the same state. They rode the cable cars, singing "The Trolley Song" to the delight of the other passengers, while the gripman accompanied them on his clanging bell. They stuffed themselves with seafood at Fisherman's Wharf, and took a boat ride under the Golden Gate Bridge to the mouth of the lovely bay, for a special reason.

That was where their grandfather, Danford Denning, had nearly lost his life on a submarine. Their father, who knew the story well, told it to them as they bobbed up and down between the city and the hills of Marin County, north of the Golden Gate:

"Your grandfather was in the Navy, aboard a new submarine. They were running tests, and the captain took it down for the first dive just outside the mouth of the bay.

"Well, they rammed into an uncharted reef. Think of being trapped far below the water, with just enough air for only a few hours!"

"Golly!" Janet shuddered. "Did they ever get back up?"

"If they hadn't we wouldn't be here, silly," Peggy said. "Go on, Daddy."

"There was panic through the whole submarine. Your grandfather said he remembered praying with all his might. One of the sailors went berserk with fear and the captain was on the point of shooting him so he wouldn't endanger the lives of all aboard, but he was finally placed under sedation and quieted down. Air was already getting stale and fear was increasing when a slight jar was felt—the boat had loosened a little! The captain carefully worked the vessel back and forth, shaking it out of the grip of the soft rock. The crew ceased to breathe, while sweat poured from every pore. Finally, with a grating noise, she was free! 'Hurrah!' the men cheered and laughed while the sub surfaced. Your grandfather often said that was the closest brush anyone could have with death."

"I remember Grandpa telling the story," Dianne said, "but being here makes it real."

Each of the girls' short coast tours was a great success. When they returned from one, it took them nearly as long to tell their mother about it—as she said—as the trip itself. They couldn't get over the fact that people as far away as Spokane not only knew them and recognized each of them but knew about them—their favorite songs, and how one liked marble cake while another preferred ice cream.

It was hard to realize, standing in front of a battery of cameras in Los Angeles, that even as they stood there their images were being projected to uncountable living rooms, some thousands of miles away. The girls knew, because they had been told, that the Welk band led the popularity parade of bands all over the United States and many parts of Canada.

"Just think," Welk told them once. "While you're up there singing, there are people in Quebec, French people, watching you. Clear on the other side of the continent. Other people are looking at you from a screened-in porch in Florida, under the palm trees. Or maybe in a penthouse, forty floors up in New York, or in a fishing village in New England."

"I don't know anybody in Florida," Janet said, and the others giggled.

"Maybe you will soon," Welk said mysteriously, but he wouldn't answer any of their questions. What he meant wasn't revealed for some months—not until the spring of 1958, when he announced at rehearsal plans to take the entire cast on a coast-to-coast personal appearance tour.

"Us, too?" Peggy asked timidly after the rehearsal.

Welk smiled. "Of course, you too. You're important members of our cast. I've talked it over with your dad, and he thinks it will be a wonderful experience for you."

"Golly!" Kathy said. "Travel! Where will we go, Mr. Welk?"

"Oh, from Aladdin's Palace to the Land of Oz, by way of the Mountains of the Moon. And all on a magic carpet!"

No amount of teasing would persuade him to tell them the itinerary. He would only say that it wasn't a long trip, about two weeks, and it would give the girls a chance to meet many new friends. Later, at home, their father brought out the list of stops.

"Milwaukee, July twenty-seventh. Next day, Cleveland. Next day, Philadelphia. Then Buffalo and Boston, and two days in New York City——"

"Hey!" Peggy cried excitedly. "New York! I'm going to see Radio City Music Hall and the Empire State Building——"

"And the United Nations," Dianne said.

"And the Statue of Liberty too," added Janet. I want to walk all the way to the top and look down at the harbor and all the ships."

"Well," said their father when he could make himself heard, "from New York we go to Atlanta, Georgia, where the peaches are. Then to Chicago, where my father used to work——"

"I want to go to Marshall Field's!" Peggy said.

"Never mind Marshall Field's. From Chicago we'll go to Minneapolis—your grandfather worked there too—and then Kansas City, and back home."

"Gee!" sighed Dianne. "It sounds wonderful. If only all of us could go—Mom, and the little kids, and all."

"It would be nice," Sis Lennon said. "But it would be too much for the little ones, DeeDee. Look at little Joe— he's only a baby, and Mimi and Billy wouldn't enjoy the traveling either. We'll go someday."

"I hope so," Dianne said. "Anyway, can we phone you every day?"

"Of course you can. And there will be so much for you to do that you won't have much time to be lonesome."

Janet, determined not to be caught napping, had already begun to haul out some of her collection of dolls. "I'll need a few dresses," she said, in a businesslike tone, "and a raincoat and umbrella, and a bathing suit, and some sports clothes, and maybe I should get a new coat——"

"Hey, now!" Bill said, laughing. "We're going on a plane, along with the whole Welk band. He hasn't chartered the *Queen Mary!*"

"I'll work out a wardrobe for each of you," Sis said. "In a pinch, you can buy a dress. And you can do your own laundry."

"Laundry?" said Peggy faintly. The thought seemed to cast a shadow on her anticipation.

"Yes, Lazybones, laundry! But there won't be any dishes to do."

Peggy brightened. "That's so, isn't it?"

The tourists were cheered by the thought that their mother would have plenty of help in the house. In the short time since the girls had made their television debut, the establishment had been swelled by a number of people who did various tasks. Two girls, Lily Mae and Maudrine, came in every day to wash and dust. Betty Sanford took charge of the flood of fan mail, opening, sorting and helping to answer it. Mrs. Wilson, a neighbor, acted as Bill's helper in managing the business end—for, after all, the Lennon sisters had reached the status of a major business enterprise—and Kay Esser took charge of the girls' large wardrobe.

Even so, two weeks is a long time for a youngster, and Janet wept openly when she said good-by to her mother and the little ones. Kathy sniffed, and even Peggy and Dianne, trying their best to be grown-up and sophisticated, found their eyes wet. But it wasn't possible to stay sad with so many exciting things happening.

Plane travel was an old story to them, but the magnificent sight of the United States from the air was an ever-new thrill. Over the desert, over the Rocky Mountains— "They look like little molehills from 'way up here!" Janet said—and on to the fertile country of the vast Central Plains, there was plenty to see.

They landed in Milwaukee, Wisconsin, on July 27. As a measure of the popularity of Welk's orchestra, their concert outdrew the enormously popular Milwaukee Braves, then world champions. "This is my country," Welk told them. "Wisconsin, Minnesota, the Dakotas—wonderful people, mostly Germans and Scandinavians. My parents are German, you know."

Plenty of Milwaukeeans knew him from the "old days" and Welk introduced the girls to people who were his friends of many years. Some had traveled hundreds of miles to hear the concert. His secretary, Lois Lamont, had been born and raised in Milwaukee, and she pointed out to the girls some of the sights of Wisconsin's biggest city.

Back in the plane, and on to Cleveland on Lake Erie. Then Philadelphia, where the girls stole some time to visit the historic shrines: Independence Hall, the Liberty Bell, the Betsy Ross house. "It's so *different* from Los Angeles!" Kathy exclaimed, as they walked down the narrow, eighteenth-century street called Elfreth's Alley, a street which looks exactly the same as it did on that day when the Liberty Bell proclaimed that the Declaration of Independence had been signed. "The streets in the old part of Philadelphia are so narrow!"

"Well, it's an old town," Peggy said. "We live in a new town."

Dianne couldn't resist showing off her knowledge. "Los Angeles is nearly as old," she said in a schoolmarmish voice. "The Spaniards built a mission there in 1781. I used to know the full name of the town but I forget."

"Pul-lease!" said Kathy, aggrieved. "No school! We're on vacation!"

On to Buffalo, then to the Big Town itself—New York City. Accustomed as they were to a big city, the girls admitted they were awed by the soaring towers, the canyon-like streets, the crowds, the roar of traffic.

"Golly!" they all said, in hushed tones over and over, as a tour of Manhattan took them to one after another of the famous places they had seen innumerable times in the movies. They didn't miss a landmark—Empire State Building, Radio City, the UN Building, Central Park, Wall Street, Fifth Avenue—everything. They even took a boat ride around the island.

Two days in New York, then south to Atlanta, another historic place. Peggy managed to acquire a "you-all" accent there in their single day's stay, but it soon rubbed off under her sisters' joking. Then back to the nation's second city, Chicago, their father's birthplace, on August 4—a visit that included a trip along the magnificent lakefront boulevards and parks.

Admittedly, they were tired by this time. After Minneapolis and Kansas City, they were glad to be on their way home. Kathy called it a vacation, but actually the four girls worked hard. It's no joke to make a hurry-hurry personal appearance tour like that.

When they landed in Los Angeles, Welk thanked each one of them for her help in making the tour a success. "You're real troupers now," he told them.

But it was so good to be home again! With the kids yanking at their dresses, and rehearsals in the evenings, things soon came back to normal. Except, of course, for the stories to tell friends, and the passing around of hundreds of pictures they had taken.

That tour was an initiation. It wasn't long before they started out again, this time on their own. They were much in demand to sing at state and county fairs throughout the country—those typically American celebrations, which are always on the lookout for typically American entertainment.

They made good in a big way on the "fair circuit."

At the Columbus, Ohio, State Fair on August 27, 28, and 29, 1958, the Lennons more than doubled the attendance record set by other top-level performers. The people of the American heartland just couldn't get enough of their singing. The Columbus fair was a barometer of their popularity, which held up in subsequent appearances.

From Columbus they went to the Youngstown-Canfield County Fair, one of the oldest county fairs in the country, dating back to 1847. Its backers call it the "biggest county fair in the world." Again they broke all attendance records. On their second visit to this fair, they broke their own previous record.

On September 10 they set records at the York Interstate Fair held at York, Pennsylvania. The records they shattered had been set by world-famous performers. They were getting used to breaking records and on three days in September, at Salt Lake City, Utah, they did it again. During those three days they gave out more than 30,000 autographed photos! At a reception they were welcomed by the Governor of Utah in the famous Gold Room of the state capitol. From Salt Lake City they flew back to Chicago, where they met Welk and appeared with his orchestra.

In the summer of 1959 the Lennon girls sang at the famed Steel Pier, which extends like a long finger into the Atlantic Ocean from the boardwalk in the resort center of Atlantic City, New Jersey. Their appearance there broke all previous attendance records, although hundreds of top-billed stars have performed in this world-renowned resort during the past century. The Lennon sisters were one of four acts which performed to a packed auditorium, where every seat and all available standing room was taken.

The majority of people visiting this resort come from New York, Philadelphia, and Baltimore, but you can meet people from almost every part of the world on any day during the height of the summer season, who are drawn by the celebrated boardwalk, the many attractions, and the foaming Atlantic which laps the long sandy beaches.

The management went all out. Every motorist entering the city saw the huge billboards bearing the girls' picture and the legend: "SEE THE LENNON SISTERS—IN

PERSON—AT THE STEEL PIER!" High overhead a plane circled, towing a mammoth streamer with the same advice.

Their appearance, from July 19 to July 25, came right in the middle of one of the hottest spells of a hot summer. Usually, people on vacation shun crowded theaters during hot weather. But not this time! The Lennons' booking there was a triumph, almost a riot. They were originally scheduled for four shows daily, but the crowds demanded, and got, six. The 8,000 seats of the Steel Pier's theater were jammed solid at every performance. Crowds stood in line for hours to buy tickets. Audiences clamored for encores.

When the girls left the pier, for relaxation or a meal, they were almost mobbed by the throngs who waited patiently at the stage door, clamoring for autographs. On several occasions the crowds were so thick that the girls' father had to appeal for a police escort. Several times, too, enthusiastic fans broke through the guard into the backstage area of the theater, and right into the sisters' dressing rooms.

It was thrilling, but a little frightening. One veteran of show business, used to deference and attention wherever he went, found himself almost ignored by the crowds waiting for the girls. Happily, the performer wasn't jealous; he became a close friend of the girls and helped make arrangements with police officials. Once, though, he remarked wryly:

"It would take me a year to give out as many autographs as those kids have in a couple of days!"

On July 26 they flew to Angola, Ind., for a county

fair. From August 3–6 they sang at the Montana State Fair at Great Falls. On August 24 another major triumph: the quartet sang with Welk's orchestra at Ak-Sar-Ben Field in Omaha, Neb., where they were cheered by a crowd estimated at 30,000. (It's interesting to note that this great crowd represented *one one-thousandth* of their weekly television audience!)

The record-breaking tour went on: September 5–8, the Nebraska State Fair at Lincoln; September 21–24, Pomona Fair, Pomona, Cal. And then back to the fall schedule of television shows.

It was an exciting, wonderful summer, and a little awe-inspiring too. Actually seeing all those thousands of people, from coast to coast, who had traveled maybe hundreds of miles just to see them in person and listen to their songs, was a terrific thrill.

But it was exhausting, too, and the girls breathed a sigh of happiness as they ran into the modest house in Venice at the summer's end. "Did you like it all?" Sis asked.

"Oh, yes!" they said in chorus. And little Janny added her own postscript:

"We liked it all fine. But I guess it's more important that they liked us."

This was just the beginning.

As the girls' popularity increased, requests for their appearances snowballed. The girls couldn't possibly fill them all. Their father and Lawrence Welk decided where they should go. Bill said:

"It's wonderful to have so many people wanting to hear the girls. If we wanted to, we could have them booked into every city in the Union. But that wouldn't be a good idea, for a number of reasons. Most important is that they're still so young. I don't want to tire them or disillusion them or give them the feeling that they're working too hard.

"The minute it appears the girls are under a strain—off go the bookings. It's a million times more important to keep them normal and enjoying themselves, and developing their own personalities, than it is to make more money. Actually, I don't care if they never earn another nickel. I want to keep the girls the way they are now."

They haven't yet reached the point of satiety. The four of them still get excited over another tour and still look forward to meeting new people.

Most important: they are still having fun. If Sis and Bill Lennon have anything to say about it, and they do, they will keep right on being good, normal, happy girls.

CHAPTER XII

Revealing Results of Kindness

Television is only a little more than a decade old and already it has set a new pattern of life in this country. Whether the pattern is for good or bad remains to be seen, but its evidence is everywhere. Go to a fishing village on the Maine coast; a cluster of adobe huts in the New Mexico desert; to southern Florida where it's summer the year around and to a Montana mountain town where it still snows in May. You'll find the same thing: a forest of spidery TV antennae, reaching out into the air for the invisible waves bringing entertainment.

House trailers have them. So do rickety backwoods shanties, many without telephones or any modern conveniences. Sometimes the TV sets and elaborate high antennae cost more than the small places which house them.

Television is an inestimable boon to the thousands of invalids, old people, or those in isolated places. It has lightened many a day of suffering for sick persons, and beguiled many a tedious hour for the lonely ones who abound in every city. TV provides a good substitute for those whose limited means or opportunity forbid travel, or for those who would never hear the great artists of music or the theater without the magic box.

Yet it isn't an unmixed blessing. Not by any means are all the offerings on television on a high level. Some of the programs are in poor taste or offensive or maudlin or overviolent or just plain dull. But then, a flick of a switch turns those programs off; and there are plenty of programs which are instructive, interesting, enjoyable, with a high degree of artistic talent.

Television has come a long, long way since those early days of 1947 and '48, when wrestling matches were the mainstay of the programming. Literally hundreds of stars have come and gone. It's pleasant to note, though, that the ones who have stayed the longest, and who apparently will last for a good long time to come, are the ones whose programs offer a combination of wholesomeness, friendliness, and unpretentiousness along with their talent.

Such a show is Lawrence Welk's, and such talent belongs to him and his cast, notably the four girls we are most interested in. They have already, in spite of their youth, become an established part of the great and complex world of television. If they choose to leave that world, it will be a choice of their own, according to their own wishes; not a choice forced on them by the fickleness of public taste.

They might so choose, even with the near certainty of a lengthy career still ahead. As previous chapters have indicated, none of the girls has had her head turned by the hullabaloo and glitter of show business. Their attitude could be summed up: "It's fun while it lasts, and while we're young. . . . But there are many more important things to think of."

Dianne will probably be the first girl to marry—naturally enough, since she's the oldest. Now in her twenty-first year, she has already had enough experience in handling household affairs. Dianne says she actually likes housework and she seems to. She's very good at all the little domestic chores, too, singing happily as she works.

Born December 1, 1939, in Los Angeles, California, Dianne is blond, blue-eyed, five feet four inches tall, and weighs 112 pounds. She likes sports and is a good golfer. She is a baseball and football fan.

Dianne is a little shy and reserved, but when she is in charge of the younger children, as she often is, they obey without question. Certainly she likes to care for the younger ones. Just watching her handle the smaller children, you know she loves them. She is calm in any situation.

Her taste in clothing is quiet. She dislikes frills and bright colors, preferring pastels, especially aqua and pink. She likes and looks well in chocolate brown. Favorite flower: gardenia.

Dianne is inclined to be a daydreamer, and likes to get away by herself (when she can!) and listen to records. She is fond of light classical music, particularly Mantovani, whose orchestra is a favorite with all the sisters. She enjoys ballads by Perry Como, Harry Belafonte, and Nat "King" Cole.

Favorite foods: spaghetti and her mother's marble cake.

Favorite song: "My Funny Valentine."

Favorite television program: Perry Como.

Her requirements for a boy friend: strong religious be-lief, fond of sports, loves children, sense of humor.

Ambition: To marry, become a wonderful wife and raise a very large family.

Dianne is a volunteer instructor for the Confraternity of Christian Doctrine.

Peggy is the one who thinks seriously of becoming a nun, but she's in no hurry to decide. "If it's God's will," she says, and believes that she will know when the time comes. She would make a good nun of a teaching order. Peggy has plenty of drive, get-up-and-go. She does house-work willingly enough, but doesn't pretend to like it—especially dishwashing. Getting out of washing dishes drives Peggy to some weird devices sometimes. Her sisters take advantage of her dislike for dishes to do her share of the washing in exchange for some other job, and it works out fine.

Born April 8, 1941 in Venice, California, Peggy has dark brown hair and brown eyes, is five feet two inches tall, and weighs 106 pounds. She is only mildly interested in sports participation, as she is not very good at it; she en-joys, however, watching baseball or football.

Peggy is friendly, vivacious, the most talkative of the four, and has lots of ambition. Her dad calls her "my take-over girl." She was an excellent student in school and is sometimes called "The Brain." Her favorite subjects were religion, English, and history. She is a stickler for punctuality.

She has a more assertive taste in clothing than Dianne, preferring brighter shades like red and green. Favorite flower: gardenia.

She's fond of classical music and especially of Ravel's *Daphnis et Chloé* and Dvořák's *New World* symphony. She also likes lighter classics, sharing the sisters' fondness for Mantovani.

Favorite food: hamburgers and cheese pizza.

Favorite songs: "Sleepy Time Down South" and "Say It Isn't So."

Favorite television program: Perry Como.

Ambition: "To do what God wants me to do and if it is His will, to become a nun."

Peggy is outgoing, has a host of friends and dates a wide circle of boys, but is at present serious about none of them. Her specifications for a boy friend are the same as Dianne's: strong religious belief, fondness for sports, love of children, sense of humor.

Her soft dark eyes speak a language of their own. If she worries, it never shows. Her warm smile wins you quickly. She looks and acts much like her mother.

Kathy is the social butterfly, who attracts boys the way a honey jug attracts bees. She's not lazy, but her mother calls her "easygoing"—things come so easily to Kathy that she doesn't need to drive very hard. Like all the girls, Kathy loves sports, especially swimming and volley ball. As is usually the case between two sisters close in age, there are frequent minor frictions between her and Peggy—notably when Kathy monopolizes the bathroom for interminable periods, which she has a habit of doing. Like Dianne, she looks forward to marriage and a large family—although she wants a college degree in education first, with a view to teaching kindergarten.

Born August 2, 1943, in Venice, California, Kathy has

dark hair and dark eyes, is five feet two inches tall, and weighs 104 pounds.

She is a combination of the traits of her two older sisters. Like Dianne, she is rather quiet; like Peggy, she is vivacious in temperament. In looks, she is closest to their mother.

Kathy does her share of the housework with no complaint, but without marked enthusiasm either. She is afflicted with a bad case of telephonitis and spends more time on the phone than any two of the others. Also, she is somewhat more preoccupied with primping and fussing. Like Dianne, her favorite colors are aqua and brown.

Kathy is a Mantovani fan, too, and likes string ensembles.

Favorite food: hamburgers, pizza, enchiladas.

Favorite songs: "You'll Never Know" and "Did I Remember?"

Favorite television program: Perry Como.

Ambition: To get a teaching degree and teach for a while, then marry and raise a family.

Plenty of boy friends, but too young to be serious about any of them.

Her ideal boy friend: kind, a sense of humor, courteous, likes sports, lives up to his religion.

Kathy looks older than her age. Her pretty head is filled with dreams. When asked which day was her happiest one, she replied, "Every day."

Janny is the sprite, the elf. She's supercharged, always seeming to be running away in six directions at once. Whatever Janet does she does at full speed and with boundless enthusiasm. She takes after Dianne in her ability at sports and will probably exceed her older sister. She's excellent at touch football, and Bill had to put his foot down sternly when she plagued him to let her play tackle football. She is generous and when a tiny girl, would give away hair-bows, toys, and even shoes to anyone who seemed to like them. Like her sisters, she envisions marriage and "about ten children." Sis and Bill can look forward to enough grandchildren to fill an average-sized school!

Born June 15, 1946, in Culver City, California. A blue-eyed blonde and growing rapidly, but in the summer of 1959 Janet was four feet ten inches tall and weighed 80 pounds.

Janny is a ball of fire, the most inquisitive and bubbly. She is very versatile; a talented singer, graceful dancer, capable actress, and an excellent natural athlete. Extremely outgoing, friendly to everyone. A good student, too, she likes spelling, English, reading, and writing.

Does her share of housework and doesn't dislike it.

In spite of her vivacity, too much praise embarrasses Janny and she runs away from it.

As might be expected, her favorite colors are red and green, instead of Dianne's subdued pastels. She shares her sisters' likes in music and television, and is an avid reader.

Favorite food: dainty snacks like meatballs, steak, baked potatoes.

Favorite song: "You'll Never Walk Alone."

Favorite TV program: Perry Como.

Ambition: To get married and have a large family.

Janny is, of course, much too young to think of boy

friends, but she has many boy friends in the sense of team mates for baseball and football games.

She has many girl friends, too, of course. She is a popular youngster; of even temperament, pleasant, and a real diplomat.

The special qualities of the four girls shine through so obviously that almost each fan has a favorite. Dianne, for her quiet dignity and poetic beauty. Peggy, for her sincere friendliness and adorable dark eyes. Kathy, for her stardust-in-the-eyes beauty. Janny, for her elfin grin and exuberance. They live a full life. The full-hour weekly show over TV, of course, necessitates many hours of rehearsal, at the studio and at home. They've made forty recordings—more studio hours, more rehearsals. As with every top personality, they are called upon to do many benefit shows for which they receive no pay. The performers' organization to which they belong limits the number of these an entertainer may appear in; otherwise, all their time would go to benefits. The girls don't begrudge these donations of time and talent for worthy causes. Benefits help build hospitals and schools, care for the ill and the aged, establish scholarships, do all manner of good, and the girls are willing to help.

They have appeared before thousands of people in theaters in trips around the country. (It's a sobering thought, though, that if they gave two theater performances a day for the rest of their lives, they would not have appeared before as many people as watch them in one TV show.)

The girls enjoy the mountains of fan mail which pour in every week. Often they express regret that they can't answer each letter personally, but that would be a super-human job. However, all the letters are answered.

Oddly, when it became known that I was interested in the girls, I began to get letters from their fans. Here is one which impressed me particularly:

JACKSON, MISS.

Mr. A. H. Parr
Glen Ellyn, Ill.

Dear Mr. Parr:

It was about two years ago that I first saw the Lennon sisters on the Lawrence Welk television show. I seldom watch TV that early in the evening because of Confessions, but this particular night I happened to be off duty and was able to enjoy the music. Well, when those four little girls walked out on the stage and began to sing, I enjoyed it more than anything else I had ever heard or seen on TV. There was just something about their manner and voices that made them seem just a little better. I was simply captivated!

After reading their story, I became one of their best fans; I always manage to see them when they perform. I enjoyed the way they had broken with teenage conventionality. There was no rocking and rolling or jerking that is so common among teenage contemporaries. They sang softly and stood almost motionless. There was a peace within them that few singers have. It was singing that one could enjoy and find relaxing. To me, it is a real contribution to the music world and, what was even more important, it was an example of what teenagers ought to strive for.

Well, to understand why I first wrote to the Lennons, one would have to understand something about my work in the parish. Since I was small, it has always been a joy helping the poor. Even though I get much credit for this work by those aware of this accomplishment, I do it because I love to do it. Everyone seems to have his pet projects—even priests.

Around the time I became interested in the Lennons, I

157

met a family here in Jackson who also had nine children. The similarity in their ages was remarkable. It was a very poor family living in three rooms. The father was out of work, the furniture about to be repossessed because payments were in default, and there were no groceries in the house. The way I met them was through a call from the mother asking for food. They were actually destitute. Naturally, I went out to do what I could and found this unfortunate situation. The children were exceptional in every way, which proved the parents were okay. It was just a bad year.

Little by little, with the help of the parish, we put them on their feet, with clothes, food and furniture. It was during this period of getting acquainted, that I learned the oldest girl had a rather deep admiration for the Lennon sisters, especially Janet. The idea occurred to me to write Janet and ask her to write the little girl and give her the feeling of importance, besides the biggest thrill of her life. Somehow, knowing something about Janet's background, I felt she would do this much to help me in my work with the new family. I wrote to Janet and gave her the whole story, and in a matter of days she came through with a very friendly letter to the little girl and to me. I don't know who was thrilled the most. That was the beginning of my friendship with the Lennons, and our letters became more frequent, and we became closer friends.

I made it possible for the children to phone the Lennons and talk with them. It was quite a thrill for everyone. I forgot to mention that the Lennon sisters sent each of the children a rosary, and prayer book for their First Communion which they personally autographed. You can imagine how these little children cherish these gifts. Mrs. Lennon also sent a check to buy their Communion outfits. So you can see what dimensions the friendship had taken.

In one of her letters and in a phone conversation, Janet had invited me to visit them. At the time, I couldn't see how I could afford such a trip, but by the time my vacation started, I had arranged for it. I felt it was going to be the happiest vacation of my life—and it turned out to be just that.

I left on July 22, because I wanted to be there on my birthday (Sis and I have the same birthday, July 25). Naturally, I was as excited as a child taking my first plane trip, and to meet such great TV stars. There were so many thrills that when I look back, I can't believe that it all happened to me.

Landing in L. A., I alighted from the plane, excited and nervous. Somehow, I had built this thing up in my mind and this was a natural reaction. And there on the runway to greet me was a simple, sweet, sleepy little Janet—just like one of my own little school children. And right away I was at home. She was so normal, my first impression was a question: How can a little girl who is so famous be so untouched by what so many people strive to obtain? My first impression remained the same, and I'm sure you, too, were given the same impressions of Janet and all the girls.

Janet then took me to meet her father Bill and right away it was as though we had known each other since childhood— the Lennons do that to you! The one thing I couldn't understand was why no one was crowding around asking for autographs. It wasn't the way I thought it would be. I felt that if they came to the airport, I would have to fight my way to see them. But as Bill explained: "The girls are not bothered too much here in the city where they live. But once they get over sixty miles out of the city, the crowds begin to form."

After this pleasant reception, Bill took me to Loyola University where I said Mass on a private altar, then we went home to meet the rest of the family. I was amazed at the way they came out to meet me; there is so much genuine humility in the children and such a reverence for the priesthood, that it just made me feel good all over. Somehow, I wasn't there any time before I was like a person who had just come home.

That afternoon we all went to the beach, where I got the worst sunburn of my life, while listening to Bill tell the whole story of the family. Here again, I noticed no one bothered the girls. Actually, I don't think they even recognized them.

That's how natural they act all the time, and that—to me—is where their real greatness lies. No put on, no acting—that's the way they are.

I noticed a very exceptional love and respect that both Bill and the children have for Sis. In fact, Bill is quick to tell you that she is really the cause of all their success. She seems to be the driving force in the family. She is not domineering, but yet she is powerful. Bill laughed and told me that whenever Sis gets angry, someone had better examine their conscience because she is always quite right.

Sincerely Yours in Christ,
(signed) FATHER EDWARD BALSER

One mother writes: "The Lennon girls have been a good influence on our six children. Their good examples carry more weight with them than we do."

Another woman writes: "We never miss the Lawrence Welk show, and look forward to hearing and seeing the Lennon sisters. They give us assurance, in the face of criticism of teen-agers, that the younger generation who will be the future America are all right. It is good to see girls as unspoiled as these four."

Another mother writes: "My eight children get along much better since they watch the Lennon sisters. It's good to see families like the Lennons."

A superintendent of a boys' school writes: "Many of my boys have the glamorous Lennon sisters' pictures as pin-ups in their rooms. Their frequent discussion of them shows they would choose their type as sweethearts."

The many compliments they receive daily would require many books, but we know that those of you who have watched and listened to them on television, know what effect they have on your emotions.

CHAPTER XIII

Lawrence Welk

No story of the four Lennon sisters would be complete without something about Lawrence Welk, their sponsor, patron, and friend. He has guided them every step of their way from an amateur quartet singing over the dinner dishes to one of the top attractions in the world of music.

Nobody really knows exactly how many people see and hear Lawrence Welk on his television shows. Conservative estimates say 25 million; liberal estimates say 35 million. Figure 30 million and you won't be far wrong.

To the average person, such a figure doesn't mean anything. You can't visualize 30 million people. You haven't seen that many people in your lifetime, whether you're twenty or seventy years of age. It's a staggering number!

Why do they all, faithfully, tune in to Lawrence's show?

There are other entertainers who have attracted a large audience—for a time. There are a few who have been in the public eye longer. Lawrence keeps on and on, with his army of fans, year after year. Ask some of them as I did, going up and down the line waiting to get into the television studio, or on trains or in the street. Their answers are often fumbling and halting, but undeniably sincere.

"Well, he never steals the show," one middle-aged woman said. "He gives others a break, especially the kids." Another, a young matron herding three excited children, said, "I'm always sure about his show. It's fun, but it's more than that, it's . . . it's . . ." She gestured, searching for a word. "It's wholesome." An elderly man said, "It's sincere. I know that sounds strange, but it's true. He means what he says. It's not just a lot of show business phoniness, and he enjoys what he's doing."

All right. He's not a show-off: he gives others a chance. He's wholesome and he's sincere. A pretty good testimonial, on the whole.

Show business (if I may be pardoned a small editorial here) is a strange life. There's no business like it, as the song says, but also there's no other career with so many pitfalls. For the weak, for the morally shaky, for the overambitious, for the greedy, show business can be a crushing misfortune. It doesn't have to be. The ranks of entertainers number many who are upright, devout, straight, charitable, wonderful people. It need hardly be added that these admirable men and women belong to all faiths. Lawrence Welk is a Roman Catholic, devout and proud of his faith; in his talented group are Protestants and Jews, and some who profess no formal beliefs at all, at least outwardly. It makes no difference to Lawrence, as long as they live up to his moral standards of honesty, courage, humbleness, and above all, charity.

He appeals to what is basically good and right, not to what is off-beat, vulgar, or wrong; he appeals to the honest human emotions of affection, humor, and warm simplicity.

It is fortunate that Dianne, Peggy, Kathy, and little Janet made their bow under his wing. Or perhaps more than fortunate—perhaps providential. What would have happened to four young girls if they had been advised to sing suggestive lyrics, sacrifice their sweetness for sensation, possibly taken, unknowingly, the road to momentary notoriety and quick oblivion?

Well, the association has been a happy one. Given the characters of the girls and of Lawrence Welk, it could hardly have been otherwise.

Welk has an unusually fine relationship with the thirty to forty members of his orchestra. The personnel changes, slowly, through the years, but most have been with him for a long time and haven't the slightest desire to go anywhere else. For men like Jerry Burke, the organist, being a member of the Lawrence Welk organization represents the fulfillment of all his ambitions.

Sometimes, as is inevitable with temperamental musicians, there are some slight tiffs and disagreements, but not many, and the wonder is that there aren't more. Usually the clouds pass quickly, and they are friends again.

This is due, at least in part, to Welk's policy of treating each member as an individual, a special talent, instead of lumping all his instrumentalists and singers together as "sidemen" or "vocalists." Each has his own dignity and each has his own following. When the orchestra is on tour, in Spokane or Chicago or Atlantic City, each member of the organization has his own personal group of fans who stand in line for hours to get an autograph or picture of their favorite.

Wisely, Welk encourages this, in contrast to some leaders who can't bear to forsake the center of the stage for a moment. How well this policy has paid off is obvious from the enormous, literally countless number of people who are his faithful admirers and fans.

In his introduction to this book, Welk comments on the sacrifices and hard work which are prerequisites to a successful musical career. His own career exemplifies that philosophy; it's worth taking a look at.

He was born in 1903, in Strasburg, North Dakota, a tiny farming town lost in the immense flat plains of the state. His parents, Ludwig and Christina Schwahn Welk, had been in the country eleven years. They were Germans who came from Russia, a fact that needs some explaining.

After the Franco-Prussian War of 1871, there were thousands of Rhineland farmers and townsmen in the Alsace-Lorraine area who were sick and tired of war, of trouble, of eternal unrest and uneasiness. The war, between France and Germany, had been won by Germany; but it was only the latest in an unending series of wars which stretched back beyond history.

That borderland, or buffer state, along the Rhine River marks the separation between two civilizations: the French-speaking world and the German-speaking world. Never, since the days of the Romans, had people living there been able to feel secure.

After the war ended in 1871, hundreds of them decided they could no longer stand the uncertainty and the dread of another conflict. They decided to pack up and move, and they did. But their choice was not wise.

Many settled in southern Russia, on the shores of the Black Sea, near the seaport city of Odessa. The land was rich and the Russian farmers friendly. The climate was good—and yet the expatriated German settlers were not happy.

They missed the beautiful green terraces and lush hills of their majestic Rhine, for one thing. But more important, they found new terror to take the place of the fear they had left. In the Russia of Czar Alexander III, who had taken over after his father's assassination, danger was everywhere. The dreaded secret police swarmed in the cities, the villages, even in the quiet countryside. A person speaking any language but Russian was a suspect. Anyone attending any church but the official state Orthodox Church was in danger. The most innocent action, the most harmless word, could be interpreted by the police as treason.

From their judgment there was no redress. Thousands were seized and sent to exile in Siberia.

Of course, under that kind of harsh oppression hatred mounted. Secret societies, favoring revolution, increased. There were daily outrages—bombings, killings, pillage, burning. On the wedding day of Ludwig Welk and Christina Schwahn in 1892, a neighbor boy came to the ceremony with news of an uprising in Odessa—an uprising that had been mercilessly put down.

Even the wedding had to be held secretly. And at the wedding feast one of the exiles, Henry Kampker, an old man loved by all, voiced the thoughts of many.

"We cannot stay here. We left our beloved Germany

to find peace and freedom, but we have found nothing but terror and oppression."

He had received a letter, the old man continued, from a relative in the United States. Somewhere in the province of North Dakota (what strange names they had in that new world!). The relative wrote that North Dakota had been admitted to the Union—Henry didn't know what that meant, but it must be something fine! Anyhow, the important thing was that the government was giving land away free to people who would settle there.

This was hard to believe. There were some objections and some incredulity. Everyone knew governments took things—they didn't give anything away! But old Henry told more about the letter. There were settlements in North Dakota, he said, of Poles, Bohemians, Scandinavians, and Irish. Everyone—and this even Henry found hard to believe—settled down and worked and didn't care whether the neighbors were Irish or Swedes.

"What are Irish and Swedes?" a small boy asked. Henry waved the question aside. It didn't matter. The point was that in North Dakota there were no revolutionary societies, no secret police, no massacres. It sounded like heaven!

Henry's enthusiasm won. At the wedding feast, while women scurried about with food and drink, and blind George Kruseman played his old accordion, the men talked in low voices about distant America. Finally, a number of the German exiles decided to go. They could see nothing ahead in Russia but trouble, terror, and sorrow.

After harvest that year the emigrants sold their farms.

The newlyweds, Ludwig and Christina Welk, along with many neighbors and friends, went to Odessa to board a sailing vessel which would take them to America. With Ludwig went the old accordion which had belonged to his blind cousin, George Kruseman—the accordion which had given them so many happy hours. Kruseman, eighty years old and tired, had given it to Ludwig before he died.

The trip was long, but made exciting by the prospect of the new life ahead. There was another new life to come, too, for Ludwig and Christina—their first child. There was a plague scare aboard the vessel, started by some nervous rumor-mongers who saw a dead horse being pitched over the side and started the report that human bodies were being cast into the sea at night, victims of the dreaded plague.

All these stories, and many more, Lawrence Welk can repeat. He heard them so many times when he was a boy that the faraway wedding in Russia is almost as vivid to him as if he had been there.

The end of the long voyage to North Dakota was a whirl of excitement. There was the Statue of Liberty and New York, the long train ride, the glad greetings from relatives who met them, the settling on their own 240-acre farm. And finally, the happiness for Ludwig and Christina that comes with a feeling of security.

North Dakota is not a mild land. The winters are harsh and cold. The summers are baking hot, punctuated with severe storms. There are cyclones, hailstorms, blizzards, drought, all the hazards of a new country. But the land was theirs and they loved it. Old Henry Kampker had been right in persuading them to make the long trip.

Into this life the sixth Welk child was born, on March 11, 1903, in the middle of a raging blizzard. Ludwig, coming back from the tiny town of Strasburg with the doctor, nearly lost his way in the bitter gale and driving snow. Leaving the team and wagon at a neighbor's a mile from home, he and the good Dr. Kramer fought their way on foot through the high drifts, getting to Christina's side just before the baby came. They named him Lawrence.

He was a farm boy. Those who have never lived on a farm think of the life as hard, exacting, and monotonous. So it is, but it is also rewarding, full of unexpected pleasures. Lawrence wasn't especially robust, but he pitched in and did his share of the never-ending farm chores—until 1911 when he was eight years old.

That year changed his life. On the morning threshing was to begin, a sudden illness struck him with agonizing pain and nausea. Ludwig rushed him to Dr. Kramer, who gave his verdict immediately: acute appendicitis. With an auto borrowed from a relative, John Klein— an auto was a rare thing in North Dakota a half-century ago—Lawrence was rushed the seventy-five miles to Bismarck. None too soon. It was touch and go, even after the emergency operation. Young Lawrence, fighting peritonitis, nearly died. As it was, the illness and the long recuperation left him weak and thin, unable to do the heavy work on the farm. It was more than a year before he could do even small tasks.

His was a lonely life during those months. The boy felt useless, idle in the midst of a hard-working family. For consolation he turned to the tiny, wheezy, old-fashioned pump organ which sat in the parlor. Christina didn't want him sitting indoors in the summer, so he took his music outdoors. Not the pump organ. Lawrence unearthed the ancient accordion which had belonged to blind George overseas. His father helped him mend it, and it became his companion.

The boy was not one of those musical geniuses like Mozart. Learning the keys, learning to coax melody from the old box was hard work. But it was a challenge and Lawrence responded. All summer long he took his accordion out under the trees, under the arching sky, and played. Morning until night. Many evenings, under the blue heavens and the Milky Way, he played until his arms ached from squeezing the heavy instrument, until his fingers were so numb he couldn't tell which keys he was pressing. He played while gradually he learned the secrets of the accordion, learned to make it speak as he would have it speak—give utterance to the music inside him.

When the first fall winds began to sweep down on the farm, his mother Christina talked about school. Lawrence shook his head. He had been studying all summer, learning what he wanted to learn—music. His accordion had been his teacher, his friend, his other self. His mind was made up. He would be a musician!

Wisely, Ludwig and Christina offered no objection. The father humored him. After all, Lawrence was still a boy, and every boy had dreams. When he grew older, he would realize that you couldn't make a living from an accordion. The music kept Lawrence happy and that was the main thing.

But, even if he was going to be a musician, Lawrence was still a farm boy and a farm boy must work. And Lawrence worked—behind the heavy plow horses, out on the wide acres. As he worked he dreamed; every dream was filled with music, the music he would make some day.

Then, when he was fifteen years old, he broke his arm in a plowing accident. A broken arm didn't stop Lawrence from playing the accordion. Nothing could do that. He practiced, even with his arm in a sling, even when it hurt him to pump the bellows. But, he feared, there might be another accident, one which would leave him unable to play. That he could not face. He was nearing manhood. It was time he began to think of making his own way in the world with his accordion.

Much as he loved the timeworn old instrument which had come from blind George, it had served its turn. He needed a new one, a glittering new accordion. An accordion is not cheap. It would cost $400. Even to a successful farmer, four hundred dollars is no small thing. Drought might come, or bruising hailstorms, or flood. Life was chancy on a North Dakota farm.

Lawrence knew all this, but he had to have the new instrument! It took him weeks to summon enough courage to ask Papa for the money. When he did, his father looked at him as if he had taken leave of his senses.

"Four hundred dollars! For a music box!" he exclaimed in surprise. "What's the matter with the one you have?"

Lawrence tried to explain. It was old, it was leaky, the keys were slow in answering his call on them. Besides, if he was going to make his living with an accordion . . .

Papa only shook his head. He didn't seem to have heard what Lawrence had said about making his living from it. "When you start farming for yourself in a few years, Lawrence, you'll need every cent you can scrape together. You'll need machines, seed—a thousand things! When you're a farmer . . ."

"But I'm not going to be a farmer!" Lawrence cried desperately. "I'm going to be a musician!"

Papa simply could not understand. He could imagine no other life than that of a farmer. Lawrence went to his mother for help. She wasn't exactly enthusiastic, but if that's what Lawrence wanted, why, that's what he would get! Together, they laid siege to Papa.

Finally, after weeks of hints, arguments and pleading, Papa gave in. All right, all right! Lawrence would get his four hundred dollars! And maybe, deep in his soul, Papa understood and approved the deep longing for music which seemingly was born in his heart.

So Lawrence got his accordion—and took one more step up the ladder which was to lead him to fame and fortune.

Lawrence Welk has never forgotten the day he bought his $400 accordion. Not until he saw its sleek beauty, not until he had rippled through the scales, did he realize just how shabby his old one was.

He thought joyously: "I'm on my way!"

And so he was. It was a long road, and a hard one. Welk did not spring to the height of fame overnight— nor would he have had it that way.

It was just after World War I—great days for popular musicians. All America was dancing. Everybody wanted to hear music: the fox trot and two-step swept the country, along with numberless fads of the moment like the maxixe, the Eagle Rock, and many more. In small towns from coast to coast, in famous ballrooms in the big cities, on a thousand college campuses, sounded the banjo, the saxophone, the trumpet, and the accordion.

Lawrence found himself caught up in this new and, for a while, strange life. It was almost like being born again. He learned to think music, to speak music, to play anything at sight. From bandstands all over the land, his accordion poured forth its cascades of melody.

A wonderful life, yes, but an easy one? No, indeed!

He can tell a thousand stories of disappointments, failures, sorrows. Sometimes he would ride all night to play three hours in a leaky barn, where no dancers showed up because of a cloudburst. Mired in gluey Iowa mud. Sitting up in a rattling, cindery day coach, practicing a new arrangement. Payless paydays. Days, sometimes, when a dime was precious. En route to play at a high school prom in Nebraska and winding up stuck in a snowdrift with a fierce prairie blizzard howling.

There were times when he thought, a little wistfully, of the North Dakota farm. But never did he think of giving up and going back. He had found his life and he loved it. It was an exciting time. Musicians talked of the great names in the orchestra world: Paul Whiteman, Wayne King, Ted Lewis, Isham Jones, Guy Lombardo.

Some day, Welk told himself, he hoped his name would be included in the list of great ones. And even if this never happened, just sitting on the bandstand, playing "Dardanella," "Avalon," or "When My Baby Smiles at Me," watching the happy faces of the dancers, was reward enough.

The world moved along. More orchestras reached the top. Radio came in and America was more music-conscious than ever. Movies began to talk and sing. Slowly Welk was gaining recognition. He was evolving that style of music peculiarly his own: the "champagne music" which has come to be identified with him, wherever people listen to dance music.

Champagne music is a good expression of his personality: cheerful, hopeful, and bouncy.

Inevitably, Lawrence Welk fell in love. This happened in the late 1920s, when he met lovely Fern Renner of Yankton, South Dakota. Musicians were not popular as prospective husbands; they were too unstable, too likely to be here today and gone tomorrow, men without roots. Against this handicap there was one great asset: Fern loved him. And so they were married in 1931.

When Fern became Mrs. Welk, she blended her life indissolubly with Lawrence's. What he wanted, she would help him get; where he wanted to go, she would go too. She has remained in the background, yet her influence over him is great. He would not, even today, think of taking a major step without finding out what Fern thinks about it.

Their marriage is a success. It has helped to open the door for Welk's professional success. It wasn't long after their marriage that his star began to rise rapidly, and soon Lawrence Welk and His Orchestra were right at the top of the musical ladder.

Children came: Shirley, now the wife of Dr. Robert

Fredricks of Los Angeles and mother of two children. Donna, the second daughter, is a social worker, and young Larry, Jr., the discoverer of the Lennon sisters, is a student at Loyola University. All three are friendly, happy people who reflect their parents' devotion and training.

The television revolution came a little over ten years ago. Almost overnight, the whole face of the entertainment industry was changed. With television, Lawrence Welk found the outlet he had been seeking all his life. Instead of a few hundred people, he could play for millions!

It still seems just a little unbelievable to him. Because Lawrence Welk is what he is, the enormous success he has achieved did not make him either conceited, smug, or arrogant. God has been good to him; God allows him to make use of his talents to make others happy and to help others. A kindly, simple philosophy—and a good one to live by.

Not long ago Lawrence Welk was walking down a street in a suburb of Los Angeles. When he can, he likes to get away for a few hours and stroll by himself, watching people. On the sidewalk he saw two small urchins in ragged jeans and pullovers. One was playing, very badly, on a mouth organ. The other was doing some funny, pitiful shuffles and hops which he apparently thought was dancing.

A cap lay upside down on the sidewalk, waiting for contributions. There weren't any. None of the passers-by paid the slightest attention to the poor little show. Until Welk came along, stopped, and watched, with a smile on his face. When they saw him the boys redoubled their efforts. They finally quit, out of breath, and Welk applauded loudly.

"That's nice, boys," he said. "I enjoyed it." He dropped a dollar into the cap.

"Golly, mister, thanks!" one of the boys said, staring at the dollar bill. Welk had gauged the amount correctly. The boys, in their own way, were entertainers; they did not seek charity. Five dollars would have meant that he felt sorry for them; a dollar could have been a tribute to their talents.

"You're welcome, boys," Welk said. "Aren't you a little young to be in show business?"

Little by little, they told him a familiar story: Daddy had gone, Mama had to work, the pennies they brought home helped. There weren't many pennies, though, one said sadly. Then he brightened. "But you liked us, didn't you, mister?"

Welk laughed. "I like your spunk and the way you help your mother. Are you going to be entertainers when you grow up?"

They sure were! Like Gene Kelly and Perry Como. "D'ya think we can?" the mouth organ player asked hopefully.

"I'm sure you can. But it'll be hard work, boys. You have to study hard in school and help your mother as much as you can. Do you go to church?" They did. "Well, keep it up. Live the way the church wants you to live. And some day you may be famous."

The boys listened, round-eyed. Before they ran off, Welk said he'd like to come back and hear them tomorrow but he mightn't have the chance, so here was another dollar, just in case. The boys didn't recognize him, of course.

A tiny incident, but typical. Will the boys ever become famous entertainers? The odds are overwhelmingly against it. But who can judge the value of a kindly word and a friendly smile? No one really knows how many people Welk has helped, not even Fern Welk, although she is as close to him as one person can be to another.

Sometimes the ones being helped aren't even aware of it at the time. Later, they know. For example:

Just a few months ago, Welk, Bill Lennon, and the four girls were sitting in the commissary of the ABC Studios in Hollywood. The girls were in high spirits about a projected birthday party and there was much giggling and poking of fun. Somehow, talk got around to the studio itself, and Bill Lennon asked Welk how long the buildings had been there.

Lawrence shook his head. "I don't really know. I know that Al Jolson made the first talking picture here more than thirty years ago. *The Jazz Singer*. Did you ever hear of it, girls?"

They all nodded. They had heard of it as something which had taken place long before they were born. Lawrence recalled some of the other great names who had worked in the same studios. Some were still great names, some were memories, pleasant or otherwise, some had vanished completely.

"These walls have seen some wonderful careers," Lawrence said. "They've seen some tragedy too; stars skidding, trying to keep on top, fighting desperately to pretend they don't know what's happening to them." He shook his head.

"Sometimes an entertainer gets to feeling he's super-human, that he doesn't have to work or practice any more. He begins to slip and blames everyone but himself. Some-times show people become conceited and arrogant, look-ing down on other people, sneering at those who try to help them. I've seen that too.

"People envy us. How many teen-agers all over the country see you singing on their television screen and wish they were you?

"You know what it feels like to have people crowding around, asking for autographs, reaching out to touch you, calling to you. It's hard to keep your sense of balance when things like that happen.

"A lot of actors and musicians couldn't. They began to take all the publicity and glitter seriously. They began swaggering and feeling they were better than the people in the audience. I heard one actor calling his audience 'peasants.'"

"Gee," DeeDee said, "I don't think we would ever feel that way, Mr. Welk."

"Of course you wouldn't. Because you have too much sense and too much goodness. Entertainers who let the flattery go to their heads are always those who don't have any balance. They think their talents, given to them by God, make them better than others. That isn't so."

He sat thoughtfully for a minute and said, "I never met anyone who wasn't better than I am in some way. And you never will either." He smiled and looked at his watch. "My gosh, look at the time, and you've been letting me sit here and sound off! Come on, kids, we've got work to do!"

They bounced up and began to chatter. As the four girls walked toward the rehearsal studio, Bill dropped behind and walked with Lawrence. "I know what you were telling the kids," he said. "They'll remember it, I'm sure."

Lawrence laughed. "It's always difficult to express the way I really feel." Bill knew that Lawrence Welk, after his forty years in show business, had learned humility and charity. And that lesson is worth more than all the money he has earned, all the fame he has gained.

Whether the Lennon girls continue as professional singers, alone or as a team, or whether they retire to private lives, they have gained greatly from their association with Lawrence Welk.

He is, to sum up, a giving person. He gives what he has, what he can. To borrow a few lines from St. Francis of Assisi:

> It is in giving that we receive.
> It is in pardoning that we are pardoned.
> It is in dying that we are born into eternal life.

CHAPTER XIV

So Passes the Glory . . .

Flick on your television as Lawrence Welk's show comes on the air. There is the familiar "bubbling" background and the smooth, persuasive music. With practiced ease, the orchestra swings from one number to the next, mixing semiclassics with up-to-the-minute "pop" tunes. The four pretty Lennon girls appear on the screen and sing, confidently and sweetly.

It all looks so easy!

Of course, if a viewer stops to think about it at all, he knows there is considerable rehearsal behind that ease and smoothness. If he has taken piano lessons as far as five-finger exercises, he realizes the years of apprenticeship that go to make a finished, professional musician.

If he is—as so many of us are—the ordinary kind of person who likes music but whose efforts are sad, at best, he thinks wryly of that elusive, almost undefinable quality called "talent."

The four Lennons have it, of course. No amount of practice will make a Van Cliburn out of a tone-deaf bumbler. But talent, by itself, is not enough; many a potentially great musical career has been ruined because a performer thought himself above the necessity of practice. The great Paderewski said once: "If I miss practice for a day, I notice it; if I miss for two days, the audiences notice it."

The modest Lennon girls would be the last ones to class themselves with such a trained musician as Van Cliburn; they listen, in wide-eyed wonder, to their hi-fi recordings by such supreme artists. But if they are not musical immortals, they are extremely talented, hard-working girls; they know the value of practice, of rehearsal, of constant trying for improvement.

Speaking for myself—a musical duffer—I was amazed and more than a little impressed to see how hard the youngsters work, under the direction of Welk and of their father, and how devotedly they seek that little extra something which sets them apart from the dozens of other sister groups.

It might be interesting to spend a week with the Lennons and observe their overcrowded schedule. They go at a pace which would wear out a strong man. It wore me out—and I'm no stranger to hard work! Yet they thrive on it. Part of it is the inexhaustible energy of youth; the observer tends to forget that these girls are so very young. Part of it is the fact that they want to make their parents and their benefactor, Lawrence Welk, proud of them— an aim at which they succeed admirably. Part of their secret is the fact that they manage to have a terrific amount of fun, even when they're working the hardest; even when they go over and over and over eight measures of a song, giving it that final professional polish.

In short, they enjoy their work. The man or woman— or boy or girl—who can say that is a lucky person.

Well, come along to the Lennon home in Venice. The week begins:

MONDAY. The whole house gets up early. They have to! With ten children, there is no time for loafing. The older ones know their duties and go about them. Kathy gets ready for school—St. Monica High, the alma mater of Dianne in 1957 and Peggy in 1959. Dianne—joined by Peggy since her graduation—help their mother with breakfast, a major chore, and with tending to the little ones. The babies and young children are used to Dianne and Peggy acting as mothers. Mimi, Joseph, and Anne Madeline, as all toddlers do, wake up early and fill the house with their demands. Janet helps supervise Pat and Billy, with whom she and Danny go to St. Mark's elementary school, just a short block away.

But even with all the "assistant mothers," morning is a prolonged hurrah until the school contingent departs. Books are lost, clothes are mislaid, milk is spilled, minor problems arise on an average of one every three minutes. All these crises have to be dealt with.

Finally, the five students are hustled off and a comparative peace descends. Only comparative, because there are still three children in the house (not, of course, counting the young ladies), and as anyone with experience knows, three children can make roughly the same amount of racket as a tribe of Comanches preparing for the warpath.

The morning mail arrives, along with the household staff. Betty Sanford, the secretary, and Dianne begin going through the mail. Most of it comes from fans, and these are set aside to be enjoyed at leisure (though Dianne is apt to get engrossed in a particularly interesting letter and have to be jogged back to duty).

Bill Lennon, meanwhile, is on the phone. There is a tremendous amount of telephoning to do in connection with the television shows, recordings, personal appearances, benefits, offers from agents or managers, and people who just call up to say "Hello."

Sis, in her self-effacing, efficient way, is supervising the work of the house and doing a good share of it herself. The preschoolers are in the yard, the baby is sleeping.

The day passes. The St. Mark's party hurries home for lunch, gobbles it and goes back to school.

A short afternoon, then the school children are back. The little boys go out into the yard, to make the day resound with their playing. Janet listens, a little wistfully; she has to do homework because there is no time after dinner. Usually, athletic Janny manages to sneak in at least a couple of innings of baseball, or a little touch football, before dinner after she has finished her homework.

Dinner—a noisy, happy family get-together. Dishes. A few minutes' relaxation. Then, for the girls, rehearsal.

This goes on in the rehearsal room, which was the inspiration of Sis. Obviously, with little children in the house, the singers had to go somewhere else. You can't rehearse properly with a baby crawling over your feet, or waking up with a wail when you reach for a high note. Sis engaged Ted Lennon and Bob Wilson to remodel the garage into an attractive paneled studio. The work was done while Bill and the girls were away on a personal appearance tour. When they returned, they found the studio—a surprise gift to Bill from Sis.

It's a pleasant place, with a fireplace flanked by shelves on which glitter the many awards, cups, trophies, and plaques the girls have won or have had presented to them. A handsome record player stands nearby, with a collection of the girls' favorites.

During rehearsal, the girls usually sit on a sofa while Bill—and occasionally his brother Pat—leads and instructs them. Rehearsal can take many forms. There might be a discussion of new numbers, with Bill interpreting the song, diction, phrasing and feeling as the composer intended. Pat understands chording and harmonies.

If they like a number, decide it fits them and can do it, they begin to try out various arrangements of harmony. They may decide it's not for them: too sophisticated, too "corny," too likely to be associated with the kind of popular music they do not care for, or not having enough harmony.

Bill Lennon uses an old pitch pipe, a veteran of years of service, and the others find their places in the chord instinctively. Sometimes they hear one and like it, or, since they are furnished publishers' lists, a new title sounds intriguing. They might find a song of bygone days which has a special appeal, a song so old that it's new. "Greensleeves," for example, a lovely haunting English melody at least four hundred years old. They might run over a song which they sang months before, just to freshen up on it.

This is fun, but it's work too. I sat there in the studio, all one evening, listening. The girls' eyes sparkle, their toes tap, as they sing a favorite song with a bounce. Sometimes they repeat a chorus, or a phrase, ten—twenty—thirty times, to get just the right "feel" of it.

Once in a while a remark by one of the girls sends them all off in a fit of giggling, and even the plaintive little "beep" of Bill Lennon's pitch pipe cannot stop the laughter for a while.

They take rest breaks, of course, for a drink of Coke, or to discuss the harmony and phrasing of a song. Sometimes Bill looks on indulgently as they give way to pure clowning—singing off key, putting absurd words to a song, or acting out some tear-jerking melodrama complete with hero, villain, and tearful Little Nell. Janet usually insists on being the villain, a part she plays with gusto.

They might spend the whole evening on one or two songs, or run through a dozen.

It's fun to listen to them. Once or twice I had the urge to add my own unmelodious baritone to their voices—an urge I suppressed, luckily. With all the byplay and the fun, this rehearsal is serious business. The girls are earning a handsome yearly income, and they feel that in return, they owe the very best performance of which they're capable.

A performance, I might add, which is very good indeed.

Rehearsal ends, and they race back to the house, chattering. A glass of milk apiece, maybe some good-natured scuffling over cookies or a piece of cake. A rush for the bathroom, to get teeth brushed and go through the before-bed routine which every woman, from ten to eighty, seems to need.

Then under the covers, and a quiet night's sleep.

TUESDAY. About the same. Except that Tuesday is usually their recording day. In the afternoon they go to the studio for production settings. The girls have made many albums and single records for Brunswick, Coral, RCA, Thesaurus, and Dot. This is no small part of their activity: the Lennon sisters' records have sold over 100,-000 albums and over 1,000,000 singles!

WEDNESDAY. Starts same as Monday. After school go for dress fittings, publicity, homework, and rehearsal of numbers to be done for Mr. Welk at Thursday rehearsal for show selection.

When they had a Wednesday show Mr. Lennon would drive them to the ABC Studios at Prospect and Talmadge, Hollywood, twenty-five miles away from their home. On the way, they stopped to pick up Mrs. Petrie, the girls' tutor, so they could keep up with their studies—no rest from schoolwork!

THURSDAY. Aragon Day. After school, Bill Lennon, with Dianne and Peggy, meets Kathy and Janet and takes them to Santa Monica's Aragon Ballroom, where Welk and his orchestra have been rehearsing since 9 A.M. This session is primarily a rehearsal for the Saturday show. The girls do not appear at the Aragon dance hall as a team, although Dianne has sung alone a number of times. When the orchestra is working without vocalists, the girls go to a side room and are put through their paces by Bill or one of the musical directors. In between times, they do homework—at least the youngest two do. Peggy, newly promoted to the exalted status of graduate, and Dianne catch up on their letter-writing.

Occasionally the girls and their father have dinner at one of the cafés on Santa Monica's famous pier, and go back for more rehearsal. If they finish early, though, they pile into the car and hurry home, to have dinner with the family—something they vastly prefer. Often, as they start out, Dianne will say gently, "We have time for a rosary."

FRIDAY. Concentrated afternoon rehearsal for the Saturday show. Also, trying out production settings and working up numbers for next week's show and the one for the following week. Can't afford to fall behind!

SATURDAY. A long, full day. Rehearsal at ABC begins at 8 A.M. A break at 12:00 for a bite to eat, then more instruction, rehearsal, practice, until the show goes on the air at 6 P.M. The girls are usually extremely tired after the show. If ever they are inclined to show a flash of temper, or get into an argument with one another, it's Saturday evening—and who can blame them?

SUNDAY. A day of blessed rest. Mass in the morning, and the rest of the day is their own unless they are scheduled to put on a benefit performance for a worthy cause. But it has to be a worthy one. Sis and Bill insist on keeping the girls free on Sunday, as far as is possible. There might be a picnic or a swim or a trip to Uncle Max's or a movie. Or just a whole day of glorious, uninterrupted resting.

Except, of course, for the routine household chores.

Then Monday again. Tough? Of course, it's tough!

There are plenty of compensations for the girls, though, and I'm not speaking, now, of the high pay. The thought that they are making friends throughout the country, that millions of people find joy in watching and listening to them, is compensation far beyond dollars.

Fortunately the entire staff of Welk's orchestra has fallen in love with the Lennons and treats each of them like a favorite kid sister. There are little birthday presents, acts of kindness, jokes, help offered in coaching. And that is compensation too.

One word more about their mother. Isabelle—Sis—prefers to keep in the background, but nonetheless she is the heart around whom the whole family revolves, from tiny Anne Madeline to Bill. Bill would be the first to admit it. She could have been a popular singer herself; Sis has a soft melodic voice. But she infinitely prefers to guide and raise a family.

If any of the children have a problem, from a skinned knee to a big decision, Sis knows it and will help. A true mother, she projects herself into her family, lives in them, rejoices when they rejoice and sorrows when they weep.

She discusses, gravely and at length, such problems as whether white or blue should be worn by the girls on their next public appearance. They listen and respect her judgment. She can, and does, cheer up a tearful Billy one minute, and next minute talk to Dianne as one adult to another.

On one thing she is adamant. Show business or no, none of her children is going to leave, by as much as one step, the path on which she is leading them, if she can help it. On that, as on most other things, she and Bill agree whole-heartedly. They have turned down fabulous offers from movie producers which would have required the girls to act in a way that, in their opinion, their girls should not act—even if it was only clustering around a juke box in a teen-age hangout, for movie purposes.

Her rule of life is simple: "Please God, let them act the way You want them to act. Whatever happens then is in Your hands. They can't possibly go wrong."

Strong love for her own and a good example keep them close to her. She is not a zealot or a fanatic, preaching on street-corners, or trying to persuade everyone to her way. But, quietly and effectively, she is teaching her children to live with God by doing His will.

It is a good way to live.

So we have spent a little time with the four Lennon sisters, their parents, and their brothers and sisters.

They are truly wonderful people. The fact that the four girls are famous is almost an accident. Had the accident not happened, they would be living just about the way they are living now. The fan mail, the autographs, the personal appearances, the money—these are incidentals.

The important thing is that Dianne, Peggy, Kathy, and Janet are being taught the right way of life. Let no one think they are angels or saints, or sweety-sweet little non-entities. They are not. They are ordinary, likable, happy, nice girls, who happen to be talented singers.